VISUALIZING DATA VISUALIZATION WITH TABLEAU AND POWER BI

A HANDS-ON GUIDE TO CREATING INSIGHTFUL AND INTERACTIVE DASHBOARDS FOR INFORMED DECISION-MAKING

Deven Roberts

COPYRIGHT

Disclaimer

The content presented in this book is for educational and informational purposes only. Every effort has been made to ensure the accuracy of the information at the time of publication; however, the author(s) and publisher make no representations or warranties about the completeness, accuracy, or current applicability of the material provided.

This book may include references to software, hardware, systems, or processes that are subject to change over time. Readers are encouraged to verify the information and ensure compatibility with their specific setups or environments before implementing any of the recommendations, instructions, or code snippets presented. Individual results may vary based on varying hardware, software versions, and user expertise.

The author(s) and publisher assume no liability for any errors, omissions, or outcomes that may arise from the application or use of the information in this book. The implementation of any techniques, processes, or configurations described herein is solely at the reader's own risk. It is recommended that users back up their data and systems and take necessary precautions before making any changes.

For complex technical challenges or if uncertainty arises, consulting with a qualified professional or technical expert is advisable.

Chapter 1: Introduction to Data Visualization

Importance of Data Visualization

Data visualization is an essential discipline in today's information-rich world. As organizations increasingly rely on data for decision-making, the ability to effectively visualize that data becomes paramount. Visualization transforms complex datasets into intuitive, visual formats, making it easier for stakeholders to understand trends, patterns, and outliers at a glance. This process not only facilitates informed decision-making but also enhances communication across various levels of an organization.

The human brain is inherently wired to process visual information more efficiently than textual data. According to studies, visuals are processed 60,000 times faster than text. This cognitive advantage makes data visualization a powerful tool, especially in contexts where rapid comprehension is critical. For example, in business meetings where decisions need to be made swiftly, presenting data visually can significantly reduce the time it takes to analyze information and reach conclusions.

Moreover, effective data visualization helps to identify correlations and causal relationships that may not be immediately apparent in raw data. By using visual tools like graphs, charts, and dashboards, analysts can present multifaceted data in a more digestible format, thus revealing insights that drive strategic initiatives. This visual approach not only aids in identifying trends but also in forecasting future outcomes based on historical data, enabling organizations to remain competitive and proactive in their respective industries.

Furthermore, data visualization plays a crucial role in storytelling with data. The narrative built around data can influence decisions and drive action. When visualizations are thoughtfully designed to tell a compelling story, they can evoke emotions and motivate stakeholders to act, making the information not just informative but persuasive.

In addition, as the volume of data generated continues to grow exponentially—often referred to as Big Data—traditional methods of analysis become insufficient. Visualization allows for the distillation of vast amounts of information into coherent visual formats, helping to uncover insights in a timely manner. In fields such as healthcare, finance, and marketing, where data is abundant and constantly evolving, visualization is not just beneficial but essential.

Lastly, the importance of data visualization extends beyond business. In public policy, journalism, and academia, effective visual representations of data can enhance public understanding of complex issues, drive advocacy, and promote transparency.

As the demand for data-driven insights rises, the ability to visualize that data effectively has become a critical skill across various sectors.

Overview of Tableau and Power BI

In the realm of data visualization, two prominent tools have emerged: Tableau and Power BI. Both of these platforms offer robust capabilities for data analysis and visualization, yet they cater to different user needs and preferences. Understanding their features and strengths is crucial for anyone looking to harness the power of data visualization.

Tableau is renowned for its user-friendly interface and powerful visualization capabilities. It enables users to create a wide array of visual representations, from basic charts to complex dashboards, with ease. Tableau's drag-and-drop functionality simplifies the process of building visualizations, making it accessible even to those without extensive technical skills. Additionally, Tableau provides a rich library of pre-built visualizations, allowing users to choose the best format for their data without starting from scratch.

One of Tableau's standout features is its ability to handle large datasets efficiently. It supports various data sources, including cloud databases, spreadsheets, and big data platforms, enabling users to analyze information from multiple angles. Tableau also excels in creating interactive dashboards, allowing viewers to engage with the data by filtering, drilling down, or exploring different aspects of the visualization. This interactivity fosters a deeper understanding of the data and promotes exploratory analysis.

Power BI, developed by Microsoft, is another leading tool in the data visualization landscape. It integrates seamlessly with other Microsoft products, such as Excel and Azure, making it a popular choice for organizations already entrenched in the Microsoft ecosystem. Power BI's interface is intuitive, with a focus on empowering users to create insights quickly. It also leverages natural language processing, allowing users to ask questions about their data in plain language and receive visualizations in response.

A significant advantage of Power BI is its affordability, particularly for organizations that already utilize Microsoft services. It offers a tiered pricing structure, including a free version that provides essential features, making it accessible for small businesses and individuals. Power BI is also known for its strong data modeling capabilities, utilizing DAX (Data Analysis Expressions) for complex calculations and aggregations.

Both Tableau and Power BI have active user communities and extensive resources available, including tutorials, forums, and user groups, fostering an environment of continuous learning and support. This community-driven aspect enhances users' ability to master the tools and share best practices.

In summary, while Tableau is favored for its advanced visualizations and interactivity, Power BI is often chosen for its integration capabilities and cost-effectiveness. The choice between the two will largely depend on an organization's specific needs, existing infrastructure, and user expertise.

Key Principles of Effective Visualization

Creating effective data visualizations requires adherence to several key principles that enhance clarity, usability, and impact. Understanding these principles can significantly improve the quality of visual representations, ensuring that the intended message is communicated effectively.

Clarity: Clarity is the cornerstone of effective visualization. The primary objective of a visualization is to convey information as clearly as possible. To achieve this, visualizations should avoid unnecessary clutter and focus on the key message. Choosing the right type of chart or graph is essential—certain visual formats are better suited for specific types of data. For instance, line graphs are ideal for showing trends over time, while bar charts are effective for comparing quantities.

Simplicity: Simplicity does not mean oversimplification; rather, it emphasizes the importance of stripping away extraneous elements that do not contribute to the message. A simple design allows viewers to focus on the data itself rather than being distracted by visual embellishments. The use of white space can help separate different elements within a visualization, making it easier to read and interpret.

Accuracy: Visualizations must accurately represent the underlying data. Misleading representations can lead to incorrect conclusions and undermine the credibility of the analysis. It is crucial to maintain appropriate scales on axes and to use consistent units of measurement. Additionally, providing context—such as baseline values or reference lines—can help clarify the significance of the data being presented.

Consistency: Consistency in design elements, such as colors, fonts, and styles, fosters familiarity and enhances comprehension. Using a cohesive color palette can also help differentiate between categories while ensuring that the overall design remains visually appealing. Consistency allows viewers to quickly understand the visual language being used, making it easier to interpret the data.

Engagement: Effective visualizations should engage viewers, prompting them to explore the data further. Incorporating interactive elements, such as filters or tooltips, can invite users to delve deeper into the information. Engagement fosters curiosity and can lead to new insights that might not have been immediately apparent.

Context: Providing context is essential for helping viewers interpret data correctly. This can include additional information such as labels, legends, or descriptive titles that explain what the visualization represents. Context helps viewers understand the significance of the data and can aid in identifying patterns or anomalies.

Storytelling: Data visualization is not just about presenting numbers; it's about telling a story with those numbers. A compelling narrative can make the data more relatable and memorable. When visualizations are designed to convey a story, they can evoke emotions and drive action. This involves considering the audience and crafting a narrative that aligns with their needs and interests.

Iteration: Finally, effective visualization is often the result of an iterative process. Initial designs may need refining based on feedback and testing. Engaging stakeholders in the design process can provide valuable insights and help ensure that the final visualization meets their needs. Iteration allows for continuous improvement, resulting in more effective visual representations over time.

By applying these key principles, data visualization practitioners can create impactful, informative, and engaging representations of data that resonate with their audience. The journey of mastering these principles can enhance not only individual skillsets but also the overall effectiveness of data-driven decision-making in organizations.

Chapter 2: Getting Started with Tableau

Installation and Setup

Getting started with Tableau begins with the installation and setup process. Tableau offers various products, including Tableau Desktop, Tableau Server, and Tableau Online. For most individual users or small teams, Tableau Desktop is the primary tool for creating visualizations and dashboards. To begin, you need to download the appropriate version from the Tableau website. Tableau provides a free trial version, allowing users to explore its capabilities before committing to a purchase.

The installation process is straightforward. After downloading the installation file, you simply need to run it and follow the on-screen prompts. Tableau Desktop is compatible with both Windows and macOS operating systems. During installation, you may be prompted to sign in to your Tableau account or create a new one. This account is essential for accessing Tableau Public and Tableau Online, where users can share and collaborate on visualizations.

Once the installation is complete, launching Tableau Desktop reveals a clean and user-friendly interface. The interface is organized into several key components, including the data pane, the worksheet area, and the dashboard area. Familiarizing yourself with these components is crucial for navigating Tableau effectively.

Before diving into visualization creation, it's important to set up your data source. Tableau supports a wide range of data connections, including files (such as Excel and CSV), databases (like SQL Server, MySQL, and Oracle), and cloud data sources (such as Google Analytics and Salesforce). Connecting to a data source involves selecting the appropriate connection type and following the prompts to access your data.

After establishing a connection, Tableau displays the data source tab, where users can preview the data and make any necessary adjustments. This includes renaming fields, changing data types, and creating calculated fields. Tableau's ability to blend multiple data sources can also enhance your analysis by allowing you to combine data from various origins into a single visualization.

With your data set up, you're ready to create your first visualization. Tableau's intuitive drag-and-drop interface allows users to easily add dimensions and measures to the view, creating visualizations in real-time. This hands-on approach makes Tableau accessible to users of all skill levels, fostering creativity and exploration.

User Interface Overview

Understanding the user interface of Tableau is key to leveraging its full potential. The interface is designed to facilitate the creation of visualizations and to enhance user experience through an intuitive layout. At the top of the interface, the menu bar contains various options, including File, Data, Worksheet, Dashboard, and Server. Each menu offers additional options tailored to specific tasks, from saving workbooks to publishing dashboards.

Below the menu bar, the toolbar provides quick access to frequently used functions, such as undo, redo, and formatting tools. This streamlined access helps users work more efficiently, reducing the need to navigate through multiple menus. Icons on the toolbar represent different visualization types, making it easy to switch between views and modify existing visualizations.

On the left side of the interface is the Data pane. This area displays all connected data sources, organized into dimensions and measures. Dimensions are categorical variables, such as names or dates, while measures are numerical values that can be aggregated. Users can drag and drop these fields into the worksheet to create visualizations. The data pane also allows for the creation of calculated fields, which can be used to derive new insights from existing data.

The central area of the interface is the worksheet area, where users build their visualizations. This is where the magic happens—visualizations take shape through simple drag-and-drop actions. As users add dimensions and measures to the view, Tableau automatically generates the most suitable visualization type. Users can further customize these visualizations through the "Show Me" panel, which suggests various chart types based on the data selected.

To the right of the worksheet area is the Marks card, a powerful tool for refining visualizations. The Marks card allows users to control various aspects of their visualizations, including color, size, shape, and label. By modifying these attributes, users can enhance the clarity and impact of their visualizations, making the data more engaging and insightful.

At the bottom of the interface, users can find the worksheet tabs, which enable navigation between multiple worksheets and dashboards within a single Tableau workbook. This organization facilitates seamless transitions between different visualizations, allowing users to present comprehensive analyses without losing context.

Additionally, Tableau offers the ability to create dashboards, which are collections of visualizations arranged on a single canvas. Dashboards allow users to present multiple perspectives on a dataset simultaneously, promoting a holistic understanding of the data. Creating a dashboard is as simple as dragging existing worksheets onto the dashboard canvas and arranging them as needed.

Familiarizing oneself with Tableau's user interface is crucial for effective visualization creation. The intuitive layout, combined with powerful features, empowers users to explore their data creatively and efficiently. As users become more comfortable navigating the interface, they can unlock advanced functionalities that enhance their data storytelling capabilities.

Connecting to Data Sources

A core strength of Tableau lies in its ability to connect to a diverse array of data sources. Understanding how to establish and manage these connections is fundamental for effective data analysis and visualization. Tableau supports a variety of connection types, catering to different user needs and data environments.

When launching Tableau, users are greeted with the "Connect" pane, which presents options for connecting to various data sources. The options are categorized into two main sections: "To a File" and "To a Server." The "To a File" category includes popular formats such as Microsoft Excel, text files (CSV), JSON, and more. For users working with offline data or smaller datasets, these file-based connections are ideal.

On the other hand, the "To a Server" section provides options for connecting to databases and cloud services. Tableau supports numerous databases, including SQL Server, MySQL, PostgreSQL, Oracle, and many others. Establishing a connection to a database typically involves entering server details, authentication credentials, and selecting the appropriate database from the list. This connection allows users to leverage larger datasets, making it suitable for organizations with extensive data repositories.

Tableau also supports live connections and extract connections. A live connection allows users to query the data source in real-time, ensuring that visualizations reflect the most current data. This is particularly useful for dynamic datasets that change frequently. However, relying on live connections may affect performance, especially with large datasets. Alternatively, extract connections enable users to create a snapshot of the data at a specific point in time. These extracts are stored locally, enhancing performance by reducing the need to query the live data source. Users can refresh extracts on a scheduled basis to ensure they remain up-to-date.

Once a connection is established, Tableau displays the data source tab, where users can preview the data and make adjustments. This preview includes a grid view of the data, allowing users to assess its structure and quality. At this stage, users can rename fields, modify data types, and perform basic data cleaning tasks. For instance, if a date field is incorrectly recognized as a string, users can change its data type to date, ensuring that visualizations behave as expected.

Tableau's data management capabilities also include the ability to blend multiple data sources. This functionality is particularly valuable when analyzing data from different origins. For example, a user might want to combine sales data from a SQL database with customer demographic data from an Excel file. By establishing relationships between these data sources, users can create comprehensive visualizations that draw insights from multiple datasets.

Additionally, Tableau allows users to create calculated fields within the data source tab. These fields enable users to perform calculations based on existing data, deriving new insights without altering the original dataset. For example, users can calculate profit margins by creating a calculated field that subtracts costs from revenues. This capability enhances the analytical power of Tableau, allowing users to customize their visualizations according to specific business needs.

Establishing and managing data connections effectively is vital for creating meaningful visualizations in Tableau. By leveraging Tableau's robust connectivity options and data management features, users can ensure their visualizations are grounded in accurate, relevant data, paving the way for insightful analysis and informed decision-making.

Chapter 3: Exploring Power BI

Installation and Setup

Getting started with Power BI involves a straightforward installation and setup process. Power BI is available in several versions, including Power BI Desktop, Power BI Pro, and Power BI Premium. For most individual users and small teams, Power BI Desktop is the primary tool used for creating reports and visualizations. It is free to download and use, making it accessible for anyone looking to analyze and visualize data.

To begin, you need to download Power BI Desktop from the official Microsoft Power BI website or the Microsoft Store. The installation process is simple: after downloading the installation file, run it and follow the prompts to complete the installation. The setup will typically involve accepting the terms of service and choosing installation options, if any are available.

Once installed, launching Power BI Desktop presents you with a clean and user-friendly interface. The layout is designed to guide users through the data import and visualization process seamlessly. The main components of the interface include the ribbon, the report canvas, the fields pane, and the visualization pane.

Upon starting Power BI Desktop, you'll first be greeted with the welcome screen, which provides options to create a new report, open existing reports, or access various resources and tutorials. Understanding this initial screen is essential as it sets the stage for the work you will be doing in Power BI.

To get started with data visualization, the next step is to connect to a data source. Power BI supports a wide array of data connections, including local files (such as Excel and CSV), databases (like SQL Server and MySQL), and online services (such as Google Analytics and SharePoint). To connect to a data source, click on the "Get Data" button on the Home ribbon, which opens a window displaying the various connection options.

After selecting your data source, you'll typically be prompted to navigate to the location of your data, enter any necessary credentials, and choose the specific tables or datasets you wish to import. Power BI allows you to preview the data before loading it, which can be useful for ensuring you're working with the correct information.

Once the data is loaded, you will find it displayed in the Fields pane on the right side of the interface. From here, you can start creating your visualizations. Power BI's drag-and-drop functionality enables you to easily add fields to the report canvas, creating visualizations in real-time as you work. This interactive approach fosters exploration and experimentation, making it easier to discover insights within your data.

In summary, the installation and setup of Power BI Desktop are designed to be user-friendly and accessible. By following the straightforward steps to download, install, and connect to data sources, users can quickly begin their journey into the world of data visualization and analysis.

User Interface Overview

Familiarizing yourself with the Power BI user interface is essential for effectively creating visualizations and reports. Power BI's design focuses on usability, ensuring that users can navigate through various functionalities with ease. The interface is divided into several key components that facilitate the data visualization process.

At the top of the screen, the ribbon is prominently displayed. The ribbon contains tabs such as Home, View, and Model, each offering a variety of options and tools for users to utilize. The Home tab, for instance, includes essential functions like importing data, creating new visualizations, and formatting options. The ribbon allows users to access commonly used features quickly, streamlining the workflow.

Central to the interface is the report canvas, which serves as the primary workspace where users create and design visualizations.

This canvas is where the magic happens; users can drag and drop fields from the Fields pane onto the report canvas to create various types of visualizations. The canvas is flexible, allowing users to arrange visual elements freely and customize the layout according to their preferences.

To the right of the report canvas is the Fields pane, which displays all the tables and fields imported from your data source. Fields are categorized as either Dimensions (categorical data) or Measures (numerical data). Users can easily identify and access their data, enabling them to build visualizations that leverage the information effectively. The Fields pane also allows for the creation of new calculated fields, enabling users to derive insights from their data dynamically.

Below the Fields pane, the Visualization pane provides a rich array of visual options. Users can choose from various chart types, such as bar charts, line graphs, pie charts, and scatter plots, as well as advanced visualizations like maps and custom visuals from the Power BI Marketplace. The Visualization pane also offers formatting options, allowing users to customize the appearance of their visualizations, including colors, labels, and titles.

Another significant component of the Power BI interface is the Filters pane. This area allows users to apply filters to their visualizations, enabling more focused analysis. By dragging fields into the Filters pane, users can limit the data displayed in their visualizations based on specific criteria. This capability enhances the interactivity of reports, allowing viewers to explore data from different angles.

Power BI also supports multiple report pages, allowing users to create comprehensive reports with different visualizations on separate pages. At the bottom of the report canvas, users can navigate between pages using the page tabs. This organization is particularly useful for presenting detailed analyses, as it allows users to separate distinct insights while maintaining a cohesive report structure.

Lastly, Power BI includes a selection of built-in themes that can be applied to reports for consistent branding and aesthetics. Users can choose from predefined themes or create custom themes to match their organization's style. This feature enhances the visual appeal of reports and helps maintain a professional look.

In summary, the Power BI user interface is designed for efficiency and ease of use. Understanding its various components—ribbon, report canvas, Fields pane, Visualization pane, Filters pane, and theme options—enables users to navigate the platform effectively and create compelling visualizations that convey insights clearly and engagingly.

Importing Data and Connecting to Sources

A fundamental aspect of using Power BI is the ability to import data from various sources and establish connections that facilitate analysis. Power BI offers a broad range of data connectivity options, catering to different user needs and environments. Understanding how to import data effectively is crucial for leveraging Power BI's capabilities to the fullest.

When starting a new report in Power BI Desktop, the process begins with selecting the "Get Data" option from the Home ribbon. This opens a window displaying various data source categories. Users can choose from file-based sources, database connections, online services, and more. This flexibility allows users to work with both structured and unstructured data, accommodating a wide array of analysis scenarios.

File-based data sources include popular formats such as Excel spreadsheets, CSV files, and text files. For example, to import data from an Excel file, users would select the Excel option, navigate to the file location, and choose the specific sheets or tables they wish to import. Power BI allows for a preview of the data, ensuring that users can confirm they are loading the correct information.

Database connections are another significant feature of Power BI. Users can connect to various databases, including SQL Server, MySQL, PostgreSQL, and Oracle, among others.

Connecting to a database typically requires entering server details, authentication credentials, and selecting the database to access. This functionality enables users to work with large datasets stored in relational databases, which can be crucial for in-depth analysis.

Power BI also supports online services, such as Google Analytics, Salesforce, and Azure services. These connections are established through OAuth or API keys, allowing users to pull in data from cloud-based platforms. This capability is especially valuable for businesses utilizing multiple cloud services, as it centralizes data analysis within Power BI.

Once a data source is connected, the next step is data transformation, often done using Power Query. Power Query is a powerful tool within Power BI that enables users to clean, reshape, and transform their data before analysis. This process is crucial for ensuring that the data is in the right format and structure for visualization.

Power Query's interface is user-friendly, featuring a series of options for modifying data. Users can remove unnecessary columns, filter rows, change data types, and even merge or append different data sources. For example, if a user imports data from an Excel sheet that contains extraneous columns, they can easily remove those columns in Power Query, streamlining the dataset for analysis.

After making the necessary transformations, users can load the cleaned data into the Power BI model. At this point, the data is ready for visualization. Users can start dragging fields onto the report canvas, creating visualizations that provide insights into the dataset.

One of Power BI's strengths is its ability to create relationships between different tables within the model. This relational capability allows users to create complex data models, enabling insights that span multiple datasets. For instance, if a user imports sales data and customer data from separate sources, they can establish a relationship based on a common key (such as Customer ID), facilitating combined analyses across both datasets.

In summary, importing data and connecting to sources in Power BI is a fundamental skill for any user. By leveraging Power BI's extensive data connectivity options and utilizing Power Query for data transformation, users can prepare their data effectively, setting the stage for impactful visualizations and analyses.

Chapter 4: Data Preparation Techniques

Understanding Data Cleaning and Transformation

Data preparation is a critical step in the data analysis process, often determining the quality and reliability of insights derived from visualizations. Before diving into visualization tools like Tableau or Power BI, it's essential to understand the concepts of data cleaning and transformation. This phase involves ensuring that your data is accurate, consistent, and in a suitable format for analysis.

Data Cleaning refers to the process of identifying and rectifying errors or inconsistencies within the dataset. Common issues that necessitate data cleaning include missing values, duplicate records, and incorrect data types. Addressing these issues is paramount, as they can lead to misleading analyses and incorrect conclusions.

For instance, missing values can arise from various sources, such as data entry errors or incomplete surveys. It's crucial to determine how to handle these missing values—options include removing rows with missing data, filling in values using techniques like imputation, or replacing them with default values. Each method has its implications, and the choice often depends on the context of the analysis.

Duplicate records present another challenge in data cleaning. These can occur due to errors in data collection or merging datasets from different sources. Identifying and removing duplicates ensures that each data point is unique, which is vital for accurate analysis. Data cleaning tools within platforms like Tableau and Power BI provide functionality for detecting and removing duplicates, streamlining this process.

In addition to missing values and duplicates, ensuring that data types are correct is essential. For example, a date field recognized as a text string can lead to improper sorting and filtering in visualizations. Proper data typing helps maintain the integrity of the data and ensures that analytical functions work as intended.

Data Transformation, on the other hand, involves modifying the data structure or format to make it more suitable for analysis. This process can include normalizing data, creating new calculated fields, and aggregating data. For instance, you might need to create a new field that calculates profit margins based on revenue and cost fields, which can then be used in visualizations to assess performance.

Normalization is another critical aspect of data transformation. This process involves adjusting values in a dataset to a common scale, which is particularly useful in comparative analyses. For example, if you're analyzing sales data across different regions, normalizing the data can help account for population size differences, providing a more equitable comparison.

Additionally, transforming categorical variables into numerical formats can facilitate certain analyses. For example, encoding categories as integers allows for mathematical operations that wouldn't be possible with string values. Similarly, splitting date fields into separate components (year, month, day) can enable more granular analyses and visualizations.

Tools like Power Query in Power BI and Tableau Prep offer robust features for data cleaning and transformation. These tools provide an intuitive interface for users to apply various data preparation techniques, often through simple drag-and-drop actions or menu selections. By mastering these features, users can significantly enhance the quality of their data, paving the way for insightful analyses.

In summary, understanding the concepts of data cleaning and transformation is crucial for anyone working with data visualization tools. By ensuring that data is accurate and properly formatted, analysts can trust the insights derived from their visualizations, ultimately leading to better-informed decision-making.

Techniques for Data Cleaning

Effective data cleaning involves a variety of techniques designed to address common data quality issues. Each technique serves a specific purpose and can significantly improve the reliability of the dataset. Here are some essential methods used in data cleaning:

Identifying and Handling Missing Values: Missing values are a common issue in datasets and can arise for various reasons, such as errors in data entry or incomplete surveys. Identifying these missing values is the first step in the cleaning process. Tools like Tableau and Power BI provide visual cues to highlight missing data, allowing users to spot issues quickly.
Once identified, analysts must decide how to handle these missing values. Common strategies include:

Deletion: Removing rows or columns with missing data. This approach can be effective when the proportion of missing data is small, but it may lead to loss of valuable information if too much data is discarded.

Imputation: Filling in missing values using statistical methods. This could involve using the mean, median, or mode of the existing data to estimate missing values, or employing more sophisticated techniques like regression or interpolation.

Flagging: Adding a new column that indicates whether a value was missing. This allows analysts to retain the original data while still accounting for the absence of values in their analyses.

Removing Duplicates: Duplicate records can skew analysis and lead to misleading insights. Identifying and removing duplicates is vital to ensure that each data point is unique. Most data visualization tools include functionality for detecting duplicates based on specific criteria, such as matching values across key columns. Once duplicates are identified, they can be removed, ensuring that the dataset reflects accurate counts and values.

Standardizing Data Formats: Inconsistent data formats can hinder analysis and lead to errors. For example, dates may be recorded in various formats (e.g., MM/DD/YYYY, DD/MM/YYYY), making it challenging to sort or filter data effectively. Standardizing data formats ensures consistency, allowing for easier analysis. This can involve converting all date formats to a single standard or ensuring that categorical data uses the same naming conventions.

Correcting Errors: Errors in data entry, such as typos or inaccuracies, can compromise the integrity of the dataset. Identifying these errors may involve cross-referencing data with original sources or conducting manual reviews. For instance, if a customer name is misspelled, it can create inconsistencies when analyzing customer-related metrics. Tools within Tableau and

Power BI can assist in highlighting anomalies, making it easier to correct errors before analysis.

Consolidating Data: When datasets originate from multiple sources, they may contain overlapping or redundant information. Consolidating data involves merging similar datasets and eliminating unnecessary duplications. This is especially useful when combining sales data from different regions or departments, ensuring that the final dataset represents a comprehensive view without redundancy.

Filtering Outliers: Outliers are extreme values that differ significantly from other observations in the dataset. While they can sometimes provide valuable insights, they can also distort analyses. Identifying and evaluating outliers is crucial; analysts should determine whether to exclude them from analyses or address them separately. Visual tools can help identify outliers, facilitating more accurate assessments of data distributions.

Validating Data Accuracy: Data validation ensures that the values within a dataset meet specific criteria or fall within expected ranges. For example, ensuring that ages are recorded as positive integers or that financial figures do not exceed logical limits can help maintain data integrity. Validation checks can be built into the data import process, providing a safety net against erroneous entries.

By employing these data cleaning techniques, analysts can significantly enhance the quality of their datasets, leading to more reliable and insightful analyses. Each technique plays a crucial role in ensuring that the data is prepared for effective visualization and decision-making.

Data Transformation Strategies

Once data is cleaned, the next step is transformation, which involves modifying the structure or format of the data to make it suitable for analysis. Various data transformation strategies can enhance the analytical power of datasets, enabling more comprehensive insights. Here are some key strategies used in data transformation:

Normalization: Normalization is the process of adjusting values in a dataset to a common scale. This is particularly important when comparing datasets that may have different units of measurement. For example, if you're analyzing sales across different regions with varying population sizes, normalizing sales figures to per capita can provide a more equitable comparison.

There are various methods for normalization, including min-max scaling, Z-score standardization, and decimal scaling. Each method has its advantages, and the choice depends on the nature of the data and the specific analytical goals.

Creating Calculated Fields: Creating calculated fields allows analysts to derive new insights from existing data. For instance, in a sales dataset, you might create a calculated field that computes profit margins based on revenue and cost figures. This new field can then be used in visualizations to assess profitability effectively.

Most data visualization tools, including Tableau and Power BI, offer built-in functionalities for creating calculated fields. These tools allow users to employ formulas and functions to generate new data points, enhancing the analytical capabilities of their datasets.

Aggregating Data: Aggregating data involves summarizing information at a higher level, such as calculating totals or averages. This strategy is particularly useful for large datasets, where individual data points may be less meaningful than overall trends. For example, instead of analyzing daily sales figures, aggregating data to show monthly or quarterly totals can reveal more significant trends and patterns.

Data visualization tools often provide options for aggregating data automatically. Users can specify the level of aggregation they desire, whether it be sums, averages, counts, or other statistical measures.

Pivoting and Unpivoting Data: Pivoting data allows analysts to reorganize the structure of a dataset for better analysis. For example, if sales data is organized by product categories and dates, pivoting the data can create a summary view that allows for easier comparisons across categories. Conversely, unpivoting data can be useful when converting wide-format data into a long format, making it suitable for certain types of analysis.

Many data preparation tools include features for pivoting and unpivoting data, enabling users to reshape their datasets without extensive manual manipulation.

Creating Hierarchies: Hierarchies are essential for drill-down analysis, allowing users to explore data at different levels of granularity. For instance, in a sales dataset, you might create a hierarchy that starts with regions, then drills down to countries, and further to cities. This hierarchical structure enables users to navigate data intuitively, exploring insights at both high and low levels.

Establishing hierarchies within data visualization tools can enhance user experience, making it easier for stakeholders to

Chapter 5: Visualizing Data with Tableau

Types of Visualizations Available in Tableau

Tableau is renowned for its wide array of visualization options, enabling users to present data in diverse and impactful ways. Understanding the different types of visualizations available is crucial for effectively conveying insights and telling a compelling story with data. Here are some of the most commonly used visualization types in Tableau:

Bar Charts: Bar charts are among the most fundamental visualizations used in Tableau. They represent categorical data with rectangular bars, where the length of each bar correlates with the value it represents. Bar charts are ideal for comparing values across different categories, making them particularly effective for analyzing sales performance across various products or regions. Tableau allows users to customize bar charts by adjusting color, size, and labels to enhance clarity and visual appeal.

Line Charts: Line charts are used to display trends over time, making them an excellent choice for time series data. They connect individual data points with lines, illustrating how values change across a continuous variable, such as dates. Line charts can effectively highlight patterns, seasonality, and trends, which are invaluable for businesses analyzing sales performance, website traffic, or any metric that varies over time.

Pie Charts: Pie charts are used to represent proportions and percentages of a whole. Each slice of the pie represents a category's contribution to the total, making them useful for visualizing market share, budget allocations, or survey results. However, it's essential to use pie charts judiciously, as they can become difficult to interpret when too many categories are present or when the differences between slices are minimal.

Scatter Plots: Scatter plots are effective for illustrating relationships between two quantitative variables. Each point on the plot represents an observation, with its position determined by the values of the two variables being compared. Scatter plots are particularly useful for identifying correlations, trends, or clusters within the data. For instance, a scatter plot can help visualize the relationship between advertising spend and sales revenue.

Heat Maps: Heat maps use color to represent data values in a matrix format, making them ideal for visualizing complex datasets with multiple dimensions. They can highlight patterns and trends that might not be immediately apparent in other visualization types. For example, a heat map can show the frequency of sales across different products and regions, using color intensity to indicate higher or lower sales volumes.

Bubble Charts: Bubble charts enhance scatter plots by adding a third dimension through the size of the bubbles. This allows users to represent an additional variable while still showing the relationship between two others. For example, in a bubble chart displaying sales data, the x-axis could represent sales volume, the y-axis could represent profit margin, and the bubble size could represent the number of units sold. This multidimensional approach provides deeper insights into the data.

Maps: Tableau offers robust mapping capabilities that allow users to visualize geographical data effectively. Maps can display various data points based on geographic dimensions, such as country, state, or city. Users can create filled maps, symbol maps, and density maps to visualize data distribution and regional trends. For example, a filled map can illustrate sales performance across different countries, providing a quick visual reference for regional strengths and weaknesses.

Dashboards: Dashboards are not a single type of visualization but rather a collection of multiple visualizations arranged on a single canvas. They allow users to present a comprehensive view of their data, combining different visualizations that provide various perspectives on the same dataset. Tableau enables users to create interactive dashboards with filters, actions, and tooltips, enhancing user engagement and exploration.

Gantt Charts: Gantt charts are specialized for project management, illustrating project timelines and progress. They display tasks along a timeline, with bars representing the duration of each task. Gantt charts are beneficial for tracking project milestones, dependencies, and overall progress, making them valuable tools for project managers and teams.

Box Plots: Box plots provide a summary of the distribution of a dataset by displaying its minimum, first quartile, median, third quartile, and maximum values. They are effective for identifying outliers and understanding the spread of data, particularly in comparative analyses. Box plots are commonly used in statistical analyses and can be particularly useful for visualizing variations across different groups or categories.

Understanding the various types of visualizations available in Tableau enables users to select the most appropriate method for presenting their data. The choice of visualization should align with the story you wish to convey and the insights you aim to highlight. By leveraging Tableau's diverse visualization options, users can create engaging, informative, and impactful representations of their data.

Creating Effective Visualizations

Creating effective visualizations in Tableau requires a thoughtful approach that considers both the data being represented and the audience consuming the information. The goal is to present insights clearly and engagingly while avoiding common pitfalls that can obscure meaning. Here are several strategies for creating effective visualizations:

Know Your Audience: Understanding your audience is crucial for tailoring your visualizations to their needs and expectations. Different stakeholders may have varying levels of data literacy and specific interests. For example, executives may prefer high-level summaries, while data analysts may seek detailed insights. By knowing your audience, you can choose the right visualization types and adjust the complexity accordingly.

Define Your Purpose: Before creating a visualization, define the key message or insight you wish to convey. Ask yourself what questions you want to answer or what story you want to tell with your data. This clarity will guide your selection of visualization types and help ensure that your visualizations align with your analytical objectives.

Choose the Right Visualization Type: Selecting the appropriate visualization type is critical for effectively conveying your message. For example, use bar charts for comparing categorical data, line charts for trends over time, and scatter plots for exploring relationships between variables. Consider the nature of your data and the insights you wish to highlight when making this choice.

Keep It Simple: Simplicity is key to effective data visualization. Avoid cluttering your visualizations with unnecessary elements that may distract from the core message. Focus on essential data points and limit the use of decorative features that do not add value. A clean, straightforward design enhances comprehension and ensures that your audience can grasp the insights quickly.

Utilize Color Wisely: Color plays a significant role in data visualization, influencing how viewers perceive and interpret information. Use color to draw attention to key data points or to differentiate between categories. However, be mindful of color choices; ensure that they are accessible to all audiences, including those with color blindness. Consider using color palettes that maintain contrast and clarity.

Incorporate Labels and Annotations: Including labels and annotations in your visualizations can provide context and enhance understanding. Use titles, axis labels, and data point labels to clarify what is being represented. Annotations can highlight specific insights or trends, guiding the audience's attention to important findings.

Leverage Interactivity: Tableau offers powerful interactivity features that can enhance the user experience. Incorporate filters, tooltips, and drill-down capabilities to allow users to explore the data on their own. Interactivity encourages engagement and can lead to deeper insights, as users can manipulate the data to answer their questions.

Test and Iterate: Visualization creation is often an iterative process. After designing your initial visualizations, gather feedback from stakeholders and consider how they interpret the information. Use this feedback to refine and improve your visualizations, ensuring that they effectively convey the intended insights.

Tell a Story with Your Data: Effective visualizations not only present data but also tell a story. Arrange your visualizations logically to guide viewers through the analysis. Use transitions and narrative techniques to create a cohesive flow, helping your audience understand the relationships between different insights.

Evaluate Performance: After deploying your visualizations, evaluate their performance in terms of user engagement and effectiveness. Analyze user interactions, such as which visualizations are most viewed or which filters are frequently used. This evaluation can inform future visualizations and help you continuously improve your data storytelling skills.

By following these strategies, users can create effective visualizations in Tableau that resonate with their audiences and convey insights clearly. The goal is to transform complex data into accessible information, enabling informed decision-making and fostering a deeper understanding of the underlying trends and patterns.

Best Practices for Dashboard Design

Dashboards serve as powerful tools for data visualization, enabling users to present multiple insights on a single canvas. Effective dashboard design is essential for ensuring that users can quickly grasp key information and make informed decisions. Here are several best practices for creating impactful dashboards in Tableau:

Define the Dashboard Purpose: Before starting the design process, clarify the primary objective of the dashboard. Determine the key metrics and insights you wish to convey, as well as the audience who will be using it. A well-defined purpose will guide your design choices and ensure that the dashboard remains focused and relevant.

Organize Information Logically: Structure your dashboard in a way that guides the user's eye through the data. Place the most critical information at the top or in prominent positions, as users typically scan dashboards from top to bottom and left to right. Group related visualizations together to provide context and facilitate comparisons.

Limit the Number of Visualizations: Avoid overwhelming users with too many visualizations on a single dashboard. Instead, focus on presenting a few key insights that directly align with the dashboard's purpose. A cluttered dashboard can lead to confusion and hinder the user's ability to interpret the information effectively.

Ensure Consistent Design: Consistency in design elements enhances user experience and reinforces the dashboard's professionalism. Use a cohesive color palette, fonts, and styles throughout the dashboard. Consistent design helps users familiarize themselves with the layout and improves their ability to interpret data.

**

Chapter 6: Visualizing Data with Power BI

Types of Visualizations Available in Power BI

Power BI is a powerful business intelligence tool that offers a wide variety of visualization options to help users represent their data effectively. Understanding the types of visualizations available is crucial for creating impactful reports and dashboards. Here are some of the most commonly used visualizations in Power BI:

Column Charts: Column charts display categorical data with vertical bars, making them ideal for comparing values across different categories. They are effective for visualizing sales data by product, revenue by region, or any scenario where comparisons are necessary. Power BI allows users to customize these charts with data labels and color schemes to enhance readability.

Line Charts: Line charts are particularly useful for showing trends over time. They connect data points with a continuous line, allowing users to observe changes and patterns across a timeline. This visualization is commonly used for metrics such as monthly sales figures, website traffic, or stock prices. Power BI provides options to add multiple lines for comparative analysis, which can help identify correlations between different datasets.

Pie and Donut Charts: Pie charts and their variation, donut charts, represent proportions of a whole. Each slice of the pie or donut corresponds to a category's share of the total. While these charts can effectively illustrate market share or budget allocation, they should be used sparingly. When categories are too numerous or the differences in proportions are minimal, pie charts can become difficult to interpret. Power BI enables users to add data labels and tooltips for better clarity.

Bar Charts: Similar to column charts, bar charts display data with horizontal bars. They are particularly effective for comparing values across categories, especially when category names are lengthy. For instance, a bar chart could effectively visualize survey results where each bar represents a different response category. Power BI offers customization options, such as sorting and coloring, to enhance the visual impact.

Scatter Plots: Scatter plots visualize the relationship between two quantitative variables. Each point represents an observation, positioned based on its values for the two variables being compared. This type of visualization is useful for identifying trends, correlations, or clusters within the data. Power BI allows users to add a third variable through bubble size, providing a multidimensional view of the data.

Map Visualizations: Power BI provides robust mapping capabilities that enable users to visualize geographical data effectively. Map visualizations can show data points based on geographic dimensions, such as countries, states, or cities. Users can create filled maps, bubble maps, and heat maps to visualize data distribution across regions. For example, a filled map can illustrate sales performance across different territories, offering insights into regional strengths and weaknesses.

Matrix Visualizations: Matrix visualizations allow users to display data in a tabular format, making it easier to view and analyze multidimensional data. They can show data across rows and columns, allowing for effective comparisons. This type of visualization is useful for presenting data such as sales figures by product category and region, providing an overview of performance across multiple dimensions.

Cards and KPIs: Cards and Key Performance Indicators (KPIs) display single data points or metrics, providing quick insights at a glance. Cards can show total sales, average revenue per user, or any other significant metric. KPIs, on the other hand, can highlight performance against a target, using visual cues such as color indicators. These visualizations are excellent for dashboards, offering users immediate access to critical information.

Waterfall Charts: Waterfall charts visualize the cumulative effect of sequentially introduced positive or negative values.

They are useful for understanding how different components contribute to a total, such as analyzing how different expenses impact overall profit. Power BI allows users to customize waterfall charts with data labels and color coding to clarify each step in the process.

Slicers: While not a standalone visualization type, slicers are essential for enhancing interactivity within reports and dashboards. They allow users to filter data dynamically based on specific criteria, such as date ranges, categories, or numeric values. Slicers enable users to explore the data in more detail, facilitating deeper insights and personalized views.

Understanding the various types of visualizations available in Power BI enables users to select the most effective method for presenting their data. The choice of visualization should align with the insights you wish to communicate and the story you want to tell. By leveraging Power BI's diverse visualization options, users can create engaging, informative, and impactful representations of their data.

Creating Effective Visualizations

Creating effective visualizations in Power BI requires careful consideration of both the data being presented and the audience consuming it. The goal is to clearly convey insights and foster understanding while avoiding common pitfalls that can lead to confusion. Here are some strategies for creating effective visualizations in Power BI:

Understand Your Audience: Knowing your audience is fundamental to tailoring your visualizations to meet their needs. Different stakeholders may have varying levels of data literacy and specific interests. For example, executives may prefer high-level summaries, while analysts may seek detailed insights. By understanding your audience, you can choose the appropriate visualization types and adjust the complexity accordingly.

Define the Key Message: Before creating a visualization, define the primary message or insight you wish to convey. Ask yourself what questions you want to answer or what story you want to tell with your data. A clear understanding of your objective will guide your selection of visualization types and help ensure that your visualizations align with your analytical goals.

Select the Right Visualization Type: Choosing the appropriate visualization type is crucial for effectively conveying your message. For instance, use bar charts for comparing categorical data, line charts for trends over time, and scatter plots for exploring relationships between variables. Consider the nature of your data and the insights you wish to highlight when making this choice.

Emphasize Clarity and Simplicity: Simplicity is key to effective data visualization. Avoid cluttering your visualizations with unnecessary elements that may distract from the core message. Focus on essential data points and limit the use of decorative features that do not add value. A clean, straightforward design enhances comprehension and ensures that your audience can quickly grasp the insights.

Utilize Color Intelligently: Color plays a significant role in data visualization, influencing how viewers perceive and interpret information. Use color to draw attention to key data points or to differentiate between categories. Be mindful of color choices; ensure that they are accessible to all audiences, including those with color blindness. Consider using color palettes that maintain contrast and clarity.

Incorporate Annotations and Tooltips: Adding annotations and tooltips to your visualizations can provide context and enhance understanding. Use titles, axis labels, and data point labels to clarify what is being represented. Tooltips can reveal additional details when users hover over data points, offering deeper insights without overcrowding the visualization.

Leverage Interactivity: Power BI's interactivity features can significantly enhance the user experience. Incorporate slicers, drill-through capabilities, and dynamic filters to allow users to explore the data on their own. Interactivity encourages engagement and can lead to deeper insights, as users can manipulate the data to answer their questions.

Iterate and Gather Feedback: Visualization creation is often an iterative process. After designing your initial visualizations, gather feedback from stakeholders to see how they interpret the information. Use this feedback to refine and improve your visualizations, ensuring that they effectively convey the intended insights.

Tell a Story with Your Data: Effective visualizations not only present data but also tell a story. Arrange your visualizations logically to guide viewers through the analysis. Use transitions and narrative techniques to create a cohesive flow, helping your audience understand the relationships between different insights.

Monitor Performance and Engagement: After deploying your visualizations, evaluate their performance in terms of user engagement and effectiveness. Analyze user interactions, such as which visualizations are most viewed or which filters are frequently used. This evaluation can inform future visualizations and help you continuously improve your data storytelling skills.

By following these strategies, users can create effective visualizations in Power BI that resonate with their audiences and convey insights clearly. The aim is to transform complex data into accessible information, enabling informed decision-making and fostering a deeper understanding of the underlying trends and patterns.

Best Practices for Dashboard Design in Power BI

Designing dashboards in Power BI involves creating a cohesive and intuitive layout that effectively communicates key insights. Following best practices can enhance the user experience and ensure that dashboards serve their intended purpose. Here are several best practices for designing effective dashboards in Power BI:

Establish a Clear Purpose: Before beginning the design process, define the primary objective of the dashboard. Determine the key metrics and insights you wish to convey, along with the audience who will be using it. A well-defined purpose will guide your design choices and ensure that the dashboard remains focused and relevant.

Organize Information Logically: Structure your dashboard in a way that guides the user's eye through the data. Place the most critical information at the top or in prominent positions, as users typically scan dashboards from top to bottom and left to right. Group related visualizations together to provide context and facilitate comparisons.

Limit the Number of Visualizations: Avoid overwhelming users with too many visualizations on a single dashboard. Instead, focus on presenting a few key insights that directly align with the dashboard's purpose. A cluttered dashboard can lead to confusion and hinder the user's ability to interpret the information effectively.

Maintain Consistent Design Elements: Consistency in design enhances user experience and reinforces the dashboard's professionalism. Use a cohesive color palette, fonts, and styles throughout the dashboard. Consistent design helps users familiarize themselves with the layout and improves their ability to interpret data.

**Utilize White Space Effect

Chapter 7: Data Preparation and Transformation

Importance of Data Preparation

Data preparation is a crucial step in the data analysis process, as it involves cleaning, transforming, and structuring raw data into a format suitable for analysis and visualization. Proper data preparation enhances the quality of insights derived from the data and minimizes the potential for errors. Here are several reasons why data preparation is essential:

Improves Data Quality: Raw data often contains inaccuracies, duplicates, and inconsistencies. Cleaning the data helps eliminate errors and ensures that the analysis is based on reliable information. High-quality data leads to more accurate insights and informed decision-making.

Facilitates Efficient Analysis: Well-prepared data is organized and structured, allowing analysts to focus on drawing insights rather than spending time correcting issues. Properly formatted data reduces the complexity of analysis, making it easier to apply analytical techniques and tools.

Enhances Visualization Effectiveness: Effective visualizations rely on clean and well-structured data. By transforming data into appropriate formats and aggregating necessary metrics, analysts can create meaningful visualizations that accurately convey insights and trends.

Supports Scalability: As organizations grow and data volumes increase, scalable data preparation processes become essential. A robust preparation workflow ensures that new data can be integrated seamlessly, maintaining the quality and consistency of analysis over time.

Prevents Misinterpretation: Poorly prepared data can lead to misinterpretation of results, which may result in misguided strategies and decisions. By ensuring data is clean and accurately represents reality, organizations can avoid costly mistakes and align their decisions with actual performance.

Steps in Data Preparation

Data preparation typically involves several key steps. Here's a structured approach to preparing data for analysis and visualization:

Data Collection: Gather data from various sources, which may include databases, spreadsheets, APIs, and external datasets. Ensuring that data sources are reliable is critical for subsequent analysis.

Data Cleaning: Identify and rectify issues in the data. Common cleaning tasks include removing duplicates, correcting errors, filling in missing values, and standardizing formats. This step is vital for enhancing data quality.

Data Transformation: Transform data into a suitable format for analysis. This may involve changing data types, aggregating values, or deriving new metrics through calculations. Transformation ensures that data aligns with the analytical objectives.

Data Integration: Combine data from multiple sources to create a comprehensive dataset. This step may involve merging tables, appending datasets, or joining data based on common fields. Integration ensures that the analysis has a holistic view of the data.

Data Enrichment: Enhance the dataset by adding additional information or context. This may include appending demographic data, geographic identifiers, or other relevant attributes that can provide deeper insights during analysis.

Data Validation: Conduct checks to ensure that the data is accurate and meets quality standards. Validation may involve cross-referencing with other datasets, applying statistical tests, or verifying with subject matter experts.

Data Structuring: Organize the data into a structured format that facilitates analysis. This may involve creating data models, defining hierarchies, or setting up relationships between tables in a database or data visualization tool.

Documentation: Document the data preparation process, including the steps taken and any transformations applied. This documentation serves as a reference for future analyses and ensures transparency in the data handling process.

Tools for Data Preparation

Numerous tools are available to assist with data preparation, each offering unique features to streamline the process. Here are some popular tools used for data preparation:

Excel: Microsoft Excel is widely used for data manipulation, offering powerful functions and features for data cleaning and transformation. It is suitable for smaller datasets and provides a user-friendly interface.

Tableau Prep: Tableau Prep is a dedicated tool for data preparation that integrates seamlessly with Tableau. It allows users to clean, combine, and transform data visually, making the process intuitive and straightforward.

Power Query: Built into Microsoft Power BI and Excel, Power Query is a powerful tool for data extraction, transformation, and loading (ETL). It enables users to connect to various data sources, apply transformations, and load the cleaned data into their analysis tools.

Alteryx: Alteryx is a robust data preparation and analytics platform that enables users to perform complex data blending and analysis without extensive coding. It offers a user-friendly interface and supports a wide range of data sources.

Python and R: For more advanced users, programming languages like Python and R provide powerful libraries for data manipulation (e.g., pandas in Python, dplyr in R). These tools allow for custom transformations and can handle large datasets efficiently.

OpenRefine: OpenRefine is a powerful tool for working with messy data. It allows users to clean, transform, and explore large datasets, making it easier to identify patterns and anomalies.

By following a structured approach to data preparation and leveraging the appropriate tools, analysts can ensure their data is clean, accurate, and ready for meaningful analysis. Proper data preparation sets the foundation for successful data visualization and insights, ultimately driving informed decision-making.

Chapter 8: Connecting to Data Sources

Understanding Data Sources in Tableau and Power BI

Connecting to various data sources is a fundamental step in using Tableau and Power BI effectively. Both platforms support a wide range of data sources, enabling users to pull in the data necessary for analysis and visualization. Understanding these data sources is essential for ensuring seamless data integration and robust reporting capabilities.

Types of Data Sources

Databases: Both Tableau and Power BI can connect to a variety of databases, including relational databases like MySQL, PostgreSQL, Oracle, and Microsoft SQL Server. Users can extract data using SQL queries, allowing for customized data retrieval and filtering.

Cloud Services: Many organizations store their data in cloud-based services. Tableau and Power BI can connect to cloud platforms like Google BigQuery, Azure SQL Database,

Amazon Redshift, and more. This connectivity allows users to work with large datasets hosted in the cloud efficiently.

Excel and CSV Files: Excel spreadsheets and CSV files are common data sources for many analysts. Both Tableau and Power BI support direct connections to these file formats, allowing users to easily import and manipulate tabular data.

Web Data Connectors: Tableau offers the ability to connect to data available on the web through Web Data Connectors (WDC). This feature allows users to pull data from web APIs and other online sources, expanding the range of available data.

REST APIs: Both platforms support connections to RESTful APIs, which allow users to pull data from various applications and services. This capability is particularly useful for integrating data from platforms like Salesforce, Google Analytics, and other cloud-based tools.

Data Warehouses: Data warehouses such as Snowflake, Google BigQuery, and Amazon Redshift provide centralized storage for large datasets. Both Tableau and Power BI can connect to these data warehouses, facilitating efficient data retrieval and analysis.

On-premises Sources: Many organizations still rely on on-premises data sources. Tableau and Power BI allow users to connect to on-premises databases and files, ensuring that analysts can access all relevant data for their projects.

Online Services: Both platforms can connect to various online services, including Microsoft SharePoint, Salesforce, and Google Analytics. These connections provide direct access to cloud-based data, enhancing the ability to analyze and visualize insights.

Connecting to Data Sources

Connecting to Data in Tableau

Open Tableau Desktop: Launch Tableau Desktop to access the start page.

Choose a Connection Type: On the left side, select the type of data source you want to connect to. Options include "Connect" to a file, server, or cloud service.

Enter Connection Details: For databases, input the necessary connection details such as server name, database name, and credentials. For files, simply navigate to the location of the file you wish to import.

Select Data: After establishing the connection, you can select specific tables or views to import into Tableau. You can also perform initial filtering or aggregations at this stage.

Data Preparation: Once the data is loaded, use Tableau's data preparation tools (like Tableau Prep) to clean and transform the data as needed.

Connecting to Data in Power BI

Open Power BI Desktop: Launch Power BI Desktop to start a new report.

Get Data: Click on the "Home" tab and select "Get Data" to see the list of available data sources.

Choose Your Source: Select the appropriate data source from the list. Power BI supports a wide variety, including databases, files, and web services.

Enter Credentials: For databases and online services, provide the necessary credentials to establish a secure connection.

Load Data: Choose the tables or data you want to load into Power BI. You can load data directly or transform it using the Power Query Editor before loading.

Data Transformation: Use the Power Query Editor to clean, shape, and transform the data before it's loaded into the Power BI model.

Best Practices for Data Connections

Optimize Data Connections: Ensure that data connections are optimized for performance. Use filters to limit the amount of data pulled in and avoid unnecessary complexity in queries.

Regularly Update Connections: Maintain regular updates to data connections, especially for dynamic data sources. Scheduled refreshes in Power BI and Tableau Server can ensure that users always access the most current data.

Use Direct Connections When Possible: Direct connections to databases allow for real-time analysis and ensure that users are working with the latest data. Where applicable, avoid using static exports unless necessary.

Secure Sensitive Data: Implement appropriate security measures when connecting to data sources. Use encryption and secure credentials to protect sensitive information and comply with data privacy regulations.

Document Data Sources: Keep thorough documentation of data sources and connection details, including any transformations applied. This documentation aids in troubleshooting and provides clarity for other analysts who may use the same data.

Test Connections Regularly: Regularly test and validate connections to ensure data integrity and availability. Any issues should be addressed promptly to prevent disruptions in reporting and analysis.

By understanding the variety of data sources available and following best practices for data connections, users can ensure a smooth and efficient workflow in both Tableau and Power BI. This foundational step is crucial for effective data analysis and visualization, ultimately leading to informed decision-making and strategic insights.

Chapter 9: Building Interactive Dashboards

Principles of Effective Dashboard Design

Creating an interactive dashboard requires a thoughtful approach that combines visual appeal with functional usability. An effective dashboard provides users with the tools they need to explore data, uncover insights, and make informed decisions. Here are key principles to consider when designing interactive dashboards in Tableau and Power BI:

Define the Dashboard Purpose

Before beginning the design process, it's essential to clearly define the dashboard's purpose. Understanding what questions the dashboard aims to answer or what insights it should convey will guide the selection of visualizations and layout. Collaborate with stakeholders to identify their specific needs and objectives, ensuring that the final product aligns with their expectations.

Focus on Key Metrics

An effective dashboard should prioritize key performance indicators (KPIs) that matter most to the audience. Avoid cluttering the dashboard with too much information. Instead, identify a few critical metrics that reflect performance, trends, and areas for improvement. Present these metrics prominently to ensure they catch the user's attention.

Use Appropriate Visualizations

Different types of visualizations serve different purposes. Choose visualizations that best represent the data and insights. For example, use line charts for trends over time, bar charts for comparisons, and pie charts for proportions. Consider the audience's familiarity with various visual types to enhance comprehension.

Ensure Clarity and Simplicity

Simplicity is key to effective dashboard design. Avoid unnecessary complexity that can overwhelm users. Use clear labels, legends, and titles to help users quickly understand what they are viewing. Minimize the use of decorative elements that do not add value to the data representation.

Leverage Interactivity

Interactivity enhances user engagement and allows for deeper exploration of the data. Incorporate features such as filters, slicers, and drill-down options to enable users to interact with the data. For example, users should be able to click on a specific region in a map to see detailed sales data for that area.

Interactivity not only helps users find relevant insights but also makes the dashboard more dynamic.

Organize Layout Logically

The layout of a dashboard should be intuitive, guiding users through the information logically. Place the most important metrics at the top or in prominent positions, allowing users to see key insights at a glance. Group related visualizations together to provide context and facilitate comparisons. A well-organized layout enhances the user experience and makes navigation easier.

Use Consistent Design Elements

Consistency in design fosters familiarity and professionalism. Use a cohesive color palette, typography, and style throughout the dashboard. Ensure that similar elements share the same formatting to maintain visual harmony. This consistency helps users quickly interpret data and understand relationships between different metrics.

Incorporate Storytelling Techniques

An effective dashboard should tell a story with the data. Use a logical flow to guide users through the insights, highlighting important trends and correlations. Consider using annotations or tooltips to provide additional context for specific data points, helping users to grasp the narrative behind the numbers.

Test and Iterate

Once the initial dashboard is designed, gather feedback from stakeholders to assess its effectiveness. Encourage users to interact with the dashboard and identify any areas for improvement. Use this feedback to iterate on the design, making necessary adjustments to enhance usability and functionality.

Steps to Build an Interactive Dashboard in Tableau

Connect to Data: Start by connecting to the relevant data sources in Tableau. Import the datasets required for your dashboard and ensure they are properly cleaned and structured.

Choose the Right Visualizations: Based on your defined metrics and audience needs, select the appropriate visualizations to represent the data effectively. Drag and drop fields onto the canvas to create visual components.

Create a Dashboard: Navigate to the Dashboard tab and create a new dashboard. Drag the individual sheets onto the dashboard canvas to assemble the visualizations. Arrange them in a logical layout that highlights key metrics.

Add Interactivity: Implement interactivity by adding filters and actions. For example, you can create filter actions that allow users to click on a chart segment to filter data across the entire dashboard. Use parameter controls to enable users to select different views or scenarios.

Incorporate Annotations: Add annotations to provide context for key data points or trends. This can enhance the storytelling aspect of the dashboard and help users understand the significance of the visualizations.

Test the Dashboard: Preview the dashboard to ensure all interactions work as intended. Gather feedback from users and make any necessary adjustments to improve clarity and usability.

Publish and Share: Once satisfied with the dashboard, publish it to Tableau Server or Tableau Online for sharing. Ensure that the appropriate permissions are set, allowing relevant stakeholders to access and interact with the dashboard.

Steps to Build an Interactive Dashboard in Power BI

Get Data: Open Power BI Desktop and click on "Get Data" to connect to your data sources. Import the necessary datasets and clean them as required in the Power Query Editor.

Create Visualizations: Use the Fields pane to drag and drop fields onto the report canvas, creating visualizations that align with your key metrics. Customize each visualization's appearance to enhance clarity.

Design the Dashboard Layout: Arrange the visualizations on the report canvas in a logical manner. Consider grouping related visuals and ensuring that the layout guides the user's eye to the most important insights first.

Add Interactivity: Incorporate slicers, drill-throughs, and other interactive elements to enhance user engagement. For example, you can add slicers to allow users to filter data by date range or categories.

Use Tooltips and Annotations: Enhance the dashboard by adding tooltips that provide additional context when users hover over data points. Annotations can also be included to highlight significant trends or insights.

Review and Test: Test the dashboard to ensure all interactive features function correctly. Solicit feedback from users to identify any areas needing improvement before finalizing the design.

Publish to Power BI Service: Once the dashboard is complete, publish it to the Power BI Service. Set up data refresh schedules and share the dashboard with stakeholders, ensuring that permissions are configured appropriately.

Conclusion

By adhering to these principles and following the steps outlined, users can build interactive dashboards in both Tableau and Power BI that not only present data effectively but also engage users in meaningful exploration. An interactive dashboard serves as a powerful tool for data-driven decision-making, allowing organizations to gain insights and respond swiftly to changing conditions.

Chapter 10: Enhancing Dashboards with Advanced Features

Utilizing Advanced Features in Tableau and Power BI

To create truly impactful dashboards, leveraging advanced features in Tableau and Power BI can significantly enhance functionality and user experience. These features provide opportunities for deeper analysis, improved interactivity, and streamlined workflows. Here's a closer look at some of these advanced capabilities and how they can be implemented in your dashboards.

Dynamic Parameters and Calculated Fields

Dynamic Parameters: Both Tableau and Power BI allow users to create dynamic parameters that can change based on user selections. This feature enhances interactivity by allowing users to select different dimensions or measures without the need to modify the underlying data source. For instance, users can choose between different sales metrics, such as total sales, average order value, or sales growth rate, all within a single parameter control.

Calculated Fields: The ability to create calculated fields is essential for deriving new insights from existing data. In Tableau, users can create calculated fields using the formula editor to perform mathematical operations, logical tests, or date calculations. Similarly, Power BI's DAX (Data Analysis Expressions) enables the creation of custom measures and calculated columns. These calculated fields can be used in visualizations to present unique insights tailored to specific analytical needs.

Drill-Down and Drill-Through Capabilities

Drill-Down: Drill-down features allow users to navigate from aggregated data to more detailed information. For example, in a sales dashboard, a user can click on a total sales figure for a specific region and drill down to view sales data by product category or individual products. This level of detail can be configured in both Tableau and Power BI by setting up hierarchies in the data model or visualization.

Drill-Through: Drill-through functionality takes users from one report or dashboard to another, providing context-specific details. For instance, clicking on a specific sales figure can lead users to a detailed report containing all transactions that contributed to that total. Setting up drill-through actions in

Power BI and Tableau enhances the user experience by offering deeper insights without cluttering the main dashboard.

Custom Visualizations and Extensions

Custom Visuals: Both Tableau and Power BI support custom visualizations that extend beyond the standard offerings. In Power BI, users can download custom visuals from the Microsoft AppSource or develop their own using the Power BI Visuals SDK. This allows for tailored visual representations suited to specific datasets or analytical requirements.

Tableau Extensions: Tableau's Extensions API enables users to integrate third-party applications or create custom functionalities within dashboards. Extensions can offer advanced capabilities such as additional data processing, enhanced interactivity, or integration with external services, enriching the dashboard experience.

Storytelling Features

Story Points in Tableau: Tableau's storytelling feature allows users to create narrative-driven dashboards that guide viewers through a sequence of visualizations. Story points can be utilized to present insights in a structured manner, making it easier for audiences to understand the data's context and implications. Users can combine different visualizations, text, and images to craft a compelling narrative.

Power BI Bookmarks: Power BI's bookmarks feature allows users to save the current state of a report, including filters, slicers, and visual configurations. Users can create a series of bookmarks to guide viewers through a presentation or analysis, enhancing storytelling capabilities. Bookmarks can be linked to buttons, enabling seamless navigation between different views or insights.

Alerts and Subscriptions

Data Alerts: Tableau and Power BI allow users to set up data alerts to notify them when certain thresholds are met or when specific conditions change. For example, a sales manager can receive alerts when sales drop below a defined level, enabling proactive decision-making. These alerts can be configured within the platforms and delivered via email or push notifications.

Subscriptions: Power BI offers subscription features that allow users to receive regular updates of reports via email. Users can subscribe to specific dashboards or reports, ensuring they stay informed about critical metrics without needing to log into the platform continuously. Tableau Server also supports similar functionalities, enhancing user engagement with the data.

Integration with Other Tools

APIs and Web Services: Both Tableau and Power BI support integrations with various external applications and services through APIs. This allows users to pull data from CRM systems, social media platforms, or other business applications. By integrating with external tools, users can enrich their dashboards with real-time data, creating a comprehensive view of performance.

Embedding Dashboards: Embedding dashboards into internal applications or websites enhances accessibility and usability. Power BI and Tableau provide options for embedding interactive dashboards within other platforms, allowing users to access critical insights directly within their workflows. This capability fosters greater engagement and promotes data-driven decision-making across the organization.

Performance Optimization

Data Optimization Techniques: Optimizing data models is essential for maintaining performance, especially as datasets grow. Both Tableau and Power BI offer tools to manage data connections and reduce the load time of dashboards. Techniques such as aggregating data, using extracts, and simplifying calculations can enhance performance, ensuring users have a seamless experience when interacting with dashboards.

Performance Monitoring: Users can monitor dashboard performance using built-in analytics tools. Tableau provides performance recording features that allow users to identify slow-loading dashboards and optimize them accordingly. Similarly, Power BI offers performance insights to analyze report responsiveness and improve user experience.

Conclusion

By incorporating these advanced features into your dashboards, you can create a more dynamic, engaging, and informative experience for users in both Tableau and Power BI. Leveraging these capabilities not only enhances the functionality of your dashboards but also empowers users to explore data in greater depth, leading to more informed decision-making and actionable insights. As data-driven decision-making becomes increasingly vital for organizations, investing time in mastering these advanced features will pay significant dividends in the quality and impact of your dashboards.

Chapter 11: Data Governance and Security

Understanding Data Governance

Data governance encompasses the management of data availability, usability, integrity, and security in an organization. Effective data governance ensures that data is accurate, consistent, and accessible while complying with regulations and safeguarding sensitive information. In the context of Tableau and Power BI, establishing robust data governance practices is essential for maintaining the integrity of dashboards and reports.

Key Components of Data Governance

Data Stewardship: Data stewards are responsible for overseeing data assets, ensuring that data is managed properly throughout its lifecycle. They define data standards, quality metrics, and procedures for data management. Establishing clear roles and responsibilities is crucial for effective stewardship, enabling accountability for data quality.

Data Quality Management: Ensuring high data quality involves regular monitoring and validation processes. Organizations should implement data quality assessments to identify inaccuracies, inconsistencies, and duplicates. Both

Tableau and Power BI provide tools to help visualize data quality issues, making it easier to address them proactively.

Data Policies and Standards: Creating clear policies and standards for data management is essential. This includes guidelines on data access, usage, and security protocols. Policies should align with industry regulations and best practices, ensuring compliance and minimizing risk.

Data Lifecycle Management: Effective data governance requires managing data throughout its lifecycle, from creation to archiving or deletion. Establishing processes for data retention, archiving, and deletion helps organizations maintain an organized and compliant data environment.

Data Cataloging: A data catalog is a centralized repository of metadata that provides information about data assets within the organization. Cataloging data enhances discoverability, making it easier for users to understand what data is available and how to access it. Both Tableau and Power BI can integrate with data cataloging tools to improve data visibility.

Data Security in Tableau and Power BI

Data security is a critical aspect of data governance, particularly as organizations increasingly rely on data for decision-making. Protecting sensitive information and ensuring that data access is appropriately controlled is essential to mitigating risks. Here are key considerations for implementing data security in Tableau and Power BI:

User Authentication and Authorization

Authentication: Establishing strong authentication mechanisms is the first step in securing data. Both Tableau and Power BI offer various authentication methods, including single sign-on (SSO), which enables users to access dashboards without needing separate credentials. Implementing multi-factor authentication (MFA) can further enhance security by requiring additional verification methods.

Authorization: Defining user roles and permissions is critical for controlling data access. Tableau and Power BI allow organizations to set up role-based access controls, ensuring that users only have access to the data and dashboards necessary for their responsibilities. This minimizes the risk of unauthorized access to sensitive information.

Data Encryption

Encrypting data at rest and in transit is vital for protecting sensitive information. Tableau and Power BI support encryption protocols to safeguard data during transmission between users and servers. Organizations should also implement encryption for stored data, ensuring that even if data is compromised, it remains unreadable without the appropriate decryption keys.

Data Masking and Anonymization

To protect sensitive data, organizations can use data masking and anonymization techniques. This involves altering or obscuring sensitive information, such as personally identifiable information (PII), so that it cannot be traced back to individuals. Tableau and Power BI allow for the implementation of these techniques, ensuring compliance with data privacy regulations.

Audit Trails and Monitoring

Maintaining audit trails of data access and changes is crucial for tracking user activity and identifying potential security breaches. Both Tableau and Power BI provide logging capabilities to capture user interactions with dashboards and reports. Regular monitoring of these logs helps organizations detect unusual activity and respond promptly to potential threats.

Regular Security Audits and Assessments

Conducting regular security audits and assessments is essential for identifying vulnerabilities in data governance and security practices. Organizations should evaluate their security measures, policies, and procedures to ensure they align with industry standards and best practices. This proactive approach enables organizations to address potential risks before they lead to data breaches or compliance issues.

Compliance with Regulations

Data governance and security practices must align with relevant regulations and industry standards. Organizations should be aware of the following regulations:

General Data Protection Regulation (GDPR): GDPR governs data protection and privacy in the European Union (EU). Organizations handling EU citizens' data must implement strict data governance practices, ensuring individuals' rights to access, rectify, and delete their data.

Health Insurance Portability and Accountability Act (HIPAA): HIPAA sets standards for protecting sensitive patient information in the healthcare industry. Organizations must ensure that their data governance and security practices comply with HIPAA regulations to safeguard patient data.

California Consumer Privacy Act (CCPA): CCPA provides California residents with rights regarding their personal information. Organizations must ensure transparency in data collection and usage practices, as well as the ability for consumers to opt out of data sales.

Payment Card Industry Data Security Standard (PCI DSS): PCI DSS outlines security measures for organizations handling credit card information. Compliance with these standards is essential for protecting payment data and maintaining customer trust.

Best Practices for Implementing Data Governance and Security

Establish a Data Governance Framework: Develop a comprehensive data governance framework that outlines roles, responsibilities, and processes for managing data. Ensure that all stakeholders understand their roles in maintaining data quality and security.

Educate Employees: Conduct regular training and awareness programs for employees regarding data governance and security policies. This includes educating staff on the importance of data privacy, security best practices, and compliance requirements.

Utilize Built-in Security Features: Take advantage of the security features available in Tableau and Power BI. Regularly review and update user access controls, encryption settings, and data governance policies to ensure they remain effective.

Document Data Governance Practices: Maintain clear documentation of data governance policies, standards, and procedures. This documentation serves as a reference for employees and supports compliance with regulatory requirements.

Continuously Monitor and Improve: Regularly review and update data governance and security practices to adapt to evolving risks and compliance requirements. Foster a culture of continuous improvement, encouraging employees to identify areas for enhancement.

Conclusion

Data governance and security are foundational elements for successful data analytics and visualization in Tableau and Power BI. By establishing robust governance frameworks and implementing effective security measures, organizations can protect sensitive information, ensure compliance with regulations, and enhance the quality of their data insights. A proactive approach to data governance not only safeguards data but also builds trust among stakeholders and empowers data-driven decision-making across the organization.

Chapter 12: Data Visualization Best Practices

Principles of Effective Data Visualization

Data visualization is an essential component of analytics, allowing users to interpret complex data sets quickly and easily. Both Tableau and Power BI offer robust visualization tools, but understanding the principles of effective data visualization is key to creating impactful dashboards. Here are best practices to guide you in designing clear, insightful, and visually appealing data representations.

Know Your Audience

Understanding your audience is crucial when designing visualizations. Different stakeholders have varying levels of familiarity with data and different information needs. Tailoring your visualizations to meet these needs can enhance comprehension and engagement. For instance, executives may prefer high-level summaries, while analysts might require detailed views and drill-down capabilities.

Choose the Right Visualization Type

Selecting the appropriate visualization type is fundamental to effectively conveying information. Here are some common visualization types and their appropriate use cases:

Bar Charts: Ideal for comparing discrete categories. Use them when you need to show differences in size across categories.

Line Charts: Best suited for displaying trends over time. They effectively communicate changes in data points across a time series.

Pie Charts: Useful for showing proportions, though they can become difficult to interpret with many categories. Limit the number of slices for clarity.

Scatter Plots: Effective for showing relationships between two continuous variables. They can help identify correlations and outliers.

Heat Maps: Great for visualizing data density or relationships across multiple dimensions. They provide quick insights into patterns and trends.

By understanding the strengths of each visualization type, you can select the most effective one for your data story.

Simplify and Focus

Simplicity is key to effective data visualization. Aim to convey your message as clearly as possible by reducing clutter and unnecessary elements. Avoid using excessive colors, fonts, or decorative elements that can distract from the data. Focus on highlighting the most important insights and metrics, allowing users to grasp the key messages quickly.

Use Color Wisely

Color can significantly impact how data is perceived. Use a consistent color scheme throughout your visualizations to create a cohesive look. Consider the following tips for using color effectively:

Limit Color Palette: Use a limited color palette to avoid overwhelming users. Stick to a few colors that complement each other and support the visualization's message.

Use Color to Convey Meaning: Use color to signify differences or highlight important data points. For example, red can indicate negative trends, while green may represent positive outcomes.

Be Mindful of Colorblind Users: Ensure that your color choices are accessible to all users, including those with color vision deficiencies. Use patterns or labels in addition to color to convey information.

Incorporate Context and Annotations

Providing context is essential for helping users understand the significance of the data. Use titles, subtitles, and axis labels to clearly describe what is being visualized. Annotations can also be valuable for highlighting key points, trends, or anomalies. These elements help users interpret the data and connect it to broader narratives.

Optimize for Interactivity

Both Tableau and Power BI offer interactive features that can enhance user engagement. Incorporating interactivity allows users to explore data on their terms, providing a more personalized experience. Consider the following interactive elements:

Filters and Slicers: Allow users to filter data based on categories or timeframes, enabling them to focus on relevant insights.

Tooltips: Use tooltips to provide additional information when users hover over data points. This can offer context without cluttering the visual.

Drill-Down Capabilities: Enable users to click on visual elements to access more detailed views, allowing for deeper exploration of the data.

Maintain Consistency

Consistency in design enhances usability and comprehension. Use the same fonts, colors, and visual styles across all dashboards and reports. This uniformity helps users familiarize themselves with the layout and navigation, making it easier to interpret the data. Additionally, consistent terminology and labels ensure clarity in communication.

Test and Iterate

Designing effective visualizations is often an iterative process. Gather feedback from stakeholders and end-users to understand their perspectives on the visualizations. Testing with real users can uncover usability issues and areas for improvement. Make adjustments based on feedback to refine the visualizations and enhance their effectiveness.

Advanced Visualization Techniques

Once you've mastered the basics, consider exploring advanced visualization techniques to elevate your dashboards further. These techniques can add depth and engagement to your data representations.

Small Multiples

Small multiples are a series of similar visualizations that allow users to compare different dimensions or time periods side by side. This technique is useful for revealing patterns or differences across categories. For instance, you could use small multiples to display sales trends for different regions over the same time frame, enabling easy comparisons.

Dashboard Storytelling

Incorporating storytelling elements into your dashboard can enhance engagement and retention of information. Use narrative techniques to guide users through the data, highlighting key insights and trends. Consider using sequential dashboards or story points to lead users through a data-driven narrative, helping them connect the dots.

Geospatial Visualizations

For data that has a geographic component, geospatial visualizations can provide valuable insights. Both Tableau and Power BI offer mapping capabilities that allow you to visualize data geographically. This can help identify trends, regional differences, or hotspots. Use maps to complement other visualizations and provide a comprehensive view of the data.

Interactive Infographics

Creating interactive infographics can combine visuals, text, and interactivity to convey complex information engagingly. Infographics can present data narratives effectively and allow users to explore various aspects of the data. By embedding interactivity, you can guide users through key insights while keeping them engaged.

Data Storytelling with Annotations

Adding annotations to your visualizations can enhance understanding by providing context or highlighting important trends. Annotations can take various forms, such as text boxes, arrows, or shapes, and can guide users' attention to critical insights. Use them strategically to clarify complex points or to draw attention to specific data trends.

Conclusion

Implementing best practices in data visualization is essential for creating dashboards that communicate insights effectively. By focusing on audience needs, choosing appropriate visualization types, simplifying designs, and incorporating interactivity, you can enhance user engagement and understanding. As you continue to explore advanced techniques, you'll be better equipped to tell compelling data stories that drive informed decision-making in your organization. Mastering data visualization is a journey that requires continuous learning and adaptation, but the rewards in clarity and impact are well worth the effort.

Chapter 13: Integrating Data from Multiple Sources

Importance of Data Integration

In today's data-driven landscape, organizations often rely on multiple data sources to gain a comprehensive view of their performance and insights. Integrating data from diverse systems—such as CRM, ERP, marketing platforms, and spreadsheets—enables more robust analytics and deeper insights. In Tableau and Power BI, effective data integration not only enhances the quality of visualizations but also supports informed decision-making.

Benefits of Integrating Data

Holistic Insights: Combining data from various sources provides a complete picture of organizational performance. This integration helps identify correlations, trends, and anomalies that may not be visible when analyzing isolated datasets.

Improved Decision-Making: When stakeholders have access to integrated data, they can make better-informed decisions. For instance, integrating sales data with marketing metrics can help assess the effectiveness of campaigns and optimize resource allocation.

Increased Efficiency: Automated data integration processes reduce manual data handling and streamline workflows. This efficiency minimizes the risk of errors and ensures that users are working with the most up-to-date information.

Enhanced Collaboration: A centralized data view fosters collaboration among teams by providing a common platform for analysis. When different departments access the same integrated data, it encourages cross-functional insights and alignment.

Data Integration Methods

To successfully integrate data from multiple sources, organizations can employ several methods, each with its advantages and challenges. Here are some common approaches:

Extract, Transform, Load (ETL)

The ETL process involves extracting data from various sources, transforming it into a suitable format, and loading it into a target database or data warehouse. ETL tools, such as Talend, Informatica, or Apache NiFi, help automate this process, ensuring that data is consistently updated and available for analysis.

Benefits:

ETL allows for extensive data cleansing and transformation, ensuring high-quality data for analysis.

It supports large volumes of data and can consolidate data from multiple sources efficiently.

Challenges:

Implementing ETL processes can be complex and require significant resources.

Data latency may occur if updates are not real-time, potentially impacting decision-making.

Data Blending

Data blending is a method used in Tableau to combine data from different sources on-the-fly. Users can create relationships between datasets without needing to perform a full ETL process. This method is particularly useful when dealing with smaller datasets or when immediate insights are required.

Benefits:

Data blending is user-friendly and does not require extensive technical expertise.

It enables quick visualizations without needing to preprocess data extensively.

Challenges:

Performance can be an issue when blending large datasets, as it relies on live connections.

Data blending may lead to inconsistent data relationships if not carefully managed.

Direct Query and Live Connections

Both Tableau and Power BI support direct queries and live connections to databases, allowing users to analyze real-time data without the need for data extraction. This method is particularly beneficial for organizations that require immediate access to up-to-date information.

Benefits:

Real-time analysis enables timely decision-making and responsiveness to changing conditions.

Users always work with the latest data, reducing the risk of using outdated information.

Challenges:

Performance may be impacted by the underlying database's speed and availability.

Not all data sources may support direct queries, limiting integration options.

Data Warehousing

Building a data warehouse involves consolidating data from multiple sources into a centralized repository designed for analysis. Data warehouses typically employ ETL processes to ensure that data is transformed and structured for efficient querying.

Benefits:

A data warehouse provides a single source of truth, promoting consistency in reporting and analysis.

It can handle large volumes of data and support complex queries, enabling in-depth analysis.

Challenges:

Implementing a data warehouse can be resource-intensive and time-consuming.

Ongoing maintenance and data governance are essential to ensure data quality and relevance.

Integrating Data in Tableau

Connecting to Multiple Data Sources

In Tableau, users can connect to various data sources, including spreadsheets, databases, and cloud services. Here's how to integrate data effectively:

Add Data Sources: In Tableau, navigate to the "Data" pane and select "Connect to Data." You can add multiple data sources by choosing the relevant connectors (e.g., Excel, SQL Server, Salesforce).

Blend Data: After connecting to multiple sources, you can create relationships between them. Tableau automatically attempts to blend data based on matching fields. You can adjust these relationships in the Data menu, ensuring that the correct joins are established.

Create Visualizations: Once the data is blended, you can create visualizations using fields from both sources. Tableau will display combined metrics, allowing for comprehensive analysis.

Using Tableau Prep

Tableau Prep is a data preparation tool that simplifies the ETL process. Users can clean, shape, and combine data before bringing it into Tableau Desktop. Key steps include:

Connect to Data: Import multiple datasets into Tableau Prep.

Transform Data: Use the intuitive interface to clean and transform data, removing duplicates and handling null values.

Output Data: Once prepared, output the cleaned data to Tableau Desktop for visualization.

Integrating Data in Power BI

Data Connection Options

Power BI offers extensive data connection options, allowing users to integrate various sources seamlessly. Follow these steps:

Get Data: Click on "Get Data" in Power BI Desktop to access a range of data sources, including databases, cloud services, and flat files.

Combine Queries: Use the Power Query Editor to combine multiple queries. This tool enables merging or appending datasets and applying transformations.

Model Relationships: In the Power BI data model, define relationships between tables. Ensure that the relationships are properly configured to support accurate data analysis.

Using Power BI Dataflows

Power BI Dataflows enable users to create reusable data preparation pipelines. This feature allows for data integration and transformation in the cloud:

Create Dataflows: In Power BI Service, create a new dataflow to connect to various sources and define transformation steps.

Schedule Refresh: Set up a refresh schedule to ensure that the data remains up-to-date.

Reuse Dataflows: Use the prepared data in multiple reports, promoting consistency and efficiency.

Best Practices for Data Integration

Define a Data Strategy: Establish a clear data integration strategy that outlines objectives, tools, and processes. This strategy should align with business goals and support effective decision-making.

Ensure Data Quality: Prioritize data quality throughout the integration process. Implement validation checks to identify and rectify data quality issues before analysis.

Document Data Sources: Maintain documentation for all integrated data sources, including their origins, transformation processes, and relationships. This documentation supports transparency and facilitates troubleshooting.

Regularly Monitor Integration Processes: Set up monitoring processes to track data integration performance and identify any issues promptly. Regular audits can help ensure that the integration processes remain effective.

Promote Collaboration Between Teams: Foster collaboration between data teams, business units, and stakeholders to ensure that the integrated data meets user needs. Involving end-users in the integration process can lead to better outcomes and increased satisfaction.

Conclusion

Integrating data from multiple sources is essential for deriving meaningful insights and making informed decisions. By employing effective integration methods in Tableau and Power BI, organizations can create a unified view of their data, driving enhanced analysis and performance. With a focus on data quality, strategic planning, and collaboration, businesses can maximize the value of their integrated data assets and improve overall decision-making processes.

Chapter 14: Dashboard Design and Layout

Fundamentals of Dashboard Design

Creating effective dashboards in Tableau and Power BI involves careful consideration of design principles, layout strategies, and user experience. A well-designed dashboard serves as a powerful tool for visualizing data, enabling users to derive insights quickly and make informed decisions. Here, we explore essential principles and best practices for dashboard design and layout.

Define the Dashboard Purpose

Before diving into design, it's crucial to clarify the dashboard's purpose. Understanding the primary objectives will guide the design process and determine the types of visualizations and data to include. Consider the following questions:

What key metrics and KPIs need to be monitored?

Who is the target audience, and what are their specific needs?

What actions or decisions should the dashboard facilitate?

By defining the purpose, you can focus on relevant data and create a more impactful dashboard.

Prioritize Key Information

A well-structured dashboard highlights the most critical information prominently. Avoid overwhelming users with excessive data; instead, prioritize essential metrics that align with the dashboard's objectives. Consider employing the "rule of three" by limiting the number of primary KPIs displayed to three to five, ensuring they stand out and are easily digestible.

Use Clear and Consistent Layouts

Maintaining a clear and consistent layout enhances usability and comprehension. Consider the following layout strategies:

Z-Pattern Layout: Human eyes naturally follow a Z-pattern when scanning a page. Place the most important information along this path, typically starting from the top left, moving to the top right, and then down to the bottom left and right.

Grid System: Utilize a grid layout to organize visual elements systematically. This approach provides balance and makes it easier for users to follow the flow of information.

Whitespace: Incorporate whitespace to prevent visual clutter. Adequate spacing around visual elements enhances readability and focuses attention on critical information.

Select Appropriate Visualizations

Choosing the right visualization types is essential for conveying data effectively. Use the following guidelines:

Use Simple Visualizations: Simple visualizations, such as bar charts or line graphs, are often more effective than complex ones. Aim for clarity over creativity, especially for presenting straightforward comparisons or trends.

Limit the Number of Visualizations: Too many visualizations can overwhelm users. Aim for a balance, ensuring that each visualization serves a purpose and contributes to the overall narrative.

Align Visualizations with Data Types: Match visualization types to the data being presented. For example, use pie charts for proportions and line charts for trends over time. This alignment enhances user comprehension.

Employ Effective Color Schemes

Color plays a vital role in dashboard design, influencing user perception and engagement. Consider the following tips for using color effectively:

Establish a Color Palette: Choose a cohesive color palette that reflects the organization's branding. Limit the number of colors to create a unified look and feel.

Use Color for Emphasis: Utilize color to highlight important metrics or trends. For example, use red to indicate negative values or green for positive trends, enhancing users' ability to interpret data quickly.

Consider Accessibility: Ensure that color choices are accessible to all users, including those with color vision deficiencies. Use patterns or text labels in addition to color to convey meaning.

Incorporate Interactive Elements

Interactive features enhance user engagement and enable deeper exploration of data. In both Tableau and Power BI, consider incorporating the following interactive elements:

Filters and Slicers: Allow users to filter data by specific criteria, enabling them to focus on relevant insights. Slicers in Power BI and filters in Tableau enhance user control over data exploration.

Tooltips: Use tooltips to provide additional context when users hover over data points. Tooltips can display details such as exact values, comparisons, or related metrics, enriching the user experience.

Drill-Down Capabilities: Enable users to click on visual elements to access more detailed information. This capability encourages exploration and helps users uncover insights that may not be immediately visible.

Optimize for Mobile Viewing

With the increasing use of mobile devices for data access, optimizing dashboards for mobile viewing is essential. Here are some considerations:

Responsive Design: Ensure that dashboards adjust well to different screen sizes. Test how visualizations render on mobile devices, making necessary adjustments to ensure readability and usability.

Simplify for Mobile: Mobile users may prefer streamlined views. Consider creating a simplified version of the dashboard with fewer visualizations and larger, touch-friendly elements.

Test and Iterate

The design process is iterative; gather feedback from users to improve the dashboard continually. Conduct usability testing to identify pain points and areas for enhancement. Use this feedback to refine layouts, adjust visualizations, and optimize the overall user experience. Regularly review and update dashboards to ensure they remain relevant and effective.

Dashboard Layout in Tableau

Creating Effective Layouts

Tableau provides a flexible canvas for designing dashboards. Consider the following steps for creating effective layouts:

Use the Dashboard Pane: Access the dashboard pane to drag and drop visualizations onto the canvas. Organize visualizations systematically to create a cohesive layout.

Use Containers: Employ horizontal and vertical containers to group related visualizations. This approach provides structure and allows for easier alignment and spacing.

Incorporate Navigation: Add navigation buttons or links to guide users between different dashboards or sections. This feature enhances usability and supports exploratory analysis.

Preview and Test: Regularly preview your dashboard during the design process to assess how visualizations interact and adjust as necessary. Test with actual users to gather feedback on usability and design.

Dashboard Layout in Power BI

Designing User-Friendly Dashboards

In Power BI, the dashboard design process involves various features and tools to enhance layout:

Grid Layout: Power BI uses a grid layout for dashboard design, allowing users to drag and position visualizations easily. Take advantage of the grid to align and organize visual elements consistently.

Bookmarks: Use bookmarks to create a series of views or scenarios within a single dashboard. This feature enables users to navigate between different visualizations or analyses seamlessly.

Responsive Design Options: Power BI offers responsive design options to ensure dashboards adapt well to various screen sizes. Utilize these settings to enhance mobile usability.

Testing and Feedback: Similar to Tableau, gather user feedback and conduct testing to refine Power BI dashboards continuously. This iterative process helps ensure that the design meets user needs.

Conclusion

Designing effective dashboards requires a thoughtful approach to layout, visualization selection, and user experience. By prioritizing key information, employing clear layouts, and incorporating interactivity, you can create dashboards that facilitate informed decision-making and enhance user engagement. As you explore the design capabilities in Tableau and Power BI, remember that continuous testing and iteration are crucial for achieving optimal results. A well-designed dashboard is not just a collection of visuals; it is a powerful tool for storytelling and data-driven insights.

Chapter 15: Advanced Analytics with Tableau and Power BI

Introduction to Advanced Analytics

In the realm of data visualization, advanced analytics refers to sophisticated techniques that enable deeper insights and predictive capabilities. Both Tableau and Power BI offer powerful features that allow users to delve beyond basic visualizations, unlocking the potential for predictive modeling, statistical analysis, and more complex data interpretations. This chapter explores the advanced analytics capabilities of these tools, focusing on techniques, applications, and best practices.

The Importance of Advanced Analytics

Advanced analytics is critical for organizations aiming to harness the full value of their data. By moving beyond traditional descriptive analytics, organizations can uncover patterns, forecast future trends, and make data-driven decisions with greater confidence. Key benefits include:

Enhanced Decision-Making: Advanced analytics equips decision-makers with predictive insights, enabling them to anticipate market shifts and customer behaviors.

Increased Efficiency: Automation of analytical processes reduces manual effort, allowing analysts to focus on strategic initiatives rather than routine data processing.

Competitive Advantage: Organizations leveraging advanced analytics can respond more quickly to changes in the market, providing them with a distinct edge over competitors.

Advanced Analytics Techniques in Tableau

Tableau offers a variety of features and techniques for performing advanced analytics. Here are some of the most notable:

Forecasting

Tableau's built-in forecasting capabilities allow users to predict future values based on historical data. This feature utilizes exponential smoothing methods, which are particularly effective for time series data.

Creating Forecasts: Users can easily add a forecast to any time-based visualization by selecting the "Forecast" option from the Analytics pane. Tableau automatically calculates forecasts based on the underlying data, providing visual indicators of forecast accuracy.

Customizing Forecasts: Users can adjust forecast settings, such as the length of the forecast period or the confidence intervals. This flexibility allows for tailoring forecasts to specific business needs.

Statistical Analysis

Tableau provides various statistical functions that empower users to perform in-depth analysis directly within their visualizations.

Trend Lines: Users can add trend lines to visualizations to display the relationship between variables. Tableau supports linear, exponential, and polynomial trend lines, offering flexibility based on data characteristics.

Clustering: Tableau allows users to create clusters, grouping similar data points based on selected dimensions. This feature is valuable for segmenting data, identifying patterns, and enhancing targeted analyses.

Correlation Analysis: Users can assess the strength and direction of relationships between variables using correlation functions. This analysis helps in identifying potential predictors and assessing data relationships.

Calculated Fields

Calculated fields enable users to create custom metrics and dimensions based on existing data. This functionality is crucial for performing complex analyses that go beyond the raw data.

Creating Calculated Fields: Users can write custom calculations using Tableau's formula language, allowing for advanced metrics like year-over-year growth, moving averages, or customer segmentation scores.

Level of Detail (LOD) Expressions: LOD expressions enable users to perform calculations at different levels of granularity. This capability is especially useful for aggregating data across dimensions that are not included in the visualization.

Advanced Analytics Techniques in Power BI

Power BI also offers robust advanced analytics capabilities, enhancing users' ability to derive insights from their data. Key features include:

DAX (Data Analysis Expressions)

DAX is a powerful formula language used in Power BI for creating custom calculations and measures. Its capabilities extend beyond basic aggregations, enabling advanced analytical functions.

Creating Measures: Users can define measures using DAX to perform calculations dynamically based on the context of the data. Examples include calculating running totals, year-over-year growth, or cohort analysis.

Time Intelligence Functions: DAX includes a suite of time intelligence functions that facilitate calculations based on date contexts, such as comparing current year data to previous years or calculating cumulative totals.

AI Insights

Power BI integrates artificial intelligence capabilities to enhance data analysis. These features empower users to leverage machine learning without requiring extensive data science expertise.

Automated Insights: Power BI's Q&A feature allows users to ask natural language questions about their data, generating insights and visualizations automatically. This capability democratizes data access, enabling non-technical users to engage with analytics.

Anomaly Detection: Power BI includes built-in anomaly detection features that identify unexpected changes in data patterns. This functionality helps users pinpoint potential issues and opportunities within their datasets.

R and Python Integration

Both Tableau and Power BI support the integration of R and Python scripts, enabling users to perform advanced statistical analysis and machine learning.

Running R Scripts: In Power BI, users can execute R scripts to perform complex analyses and visualize results within the tool. This integration expands analytical capabilities significantly, allowing for custom statistical modeling and data manipulation.

Using Python for Analytics: Similarly, Tableau allows the use of Python scripts to leverage libraries like Pandas and NumPy for data manipulation and analysis. Users can import results back into Tableau for visualization.

Best Practices for Advanced Analytics

Define Clear Objectives: Before diving into advanced analytics, establish clear objectives for what insights you aim to achieve. This focus will guide your analytical approach and ensure that efforts align with business goals.

Ensure Data Quality: High-quality data is fundamental to accurate analysis. Implement robust data governance practices to maintain data integrity, validity, and reliability.

Iterate and Refine: Advanced analytics often requires an iterative approach. Continuously refine your models and analyses based on feedback and new data to improve accuracy and relevance.

Collaborate Across Teams: Encourage collaboration between data analysts, business users, and IT teams. This collaboration fosters a shared understanding of data insights and ensures that analytical efforts meet organizational needs.

Educate Stakeholders: Ensure that stakeholders understand advanced analytics capabilities and the insights derived from analyses. Providing training and resources can empower teams to make data-driven decisions confidently.

Conclusion

Advanced analytics in Tableau and Power BI enables organizations to uncover deeper insights and make informed decisions based on predictive modeling, statistical analysis, and more complex interpretations of data. By leveraging the advanced features of these tools, users can enhance their analytical capabilities and drive better business outcomes. As organizations continue to prioritize data-driven strategies, embracing advanced analytics will be crucial for staying competitive and responsive in a rapidly changing landscape.

Chapter 16: Best Practices for Data Visualization

Understanding Data Visualization

Data visualization is a powerful means of communicating information clearly and effectively. It transforms complex data sets into graphical formats, making it easier to spot trends, patterns, and insights. However, to maximize the impact of visualizations, adhering to best practices is essential. This chapter outlines key principles and practices that enhance data visualization quality in Tableau and Power BI.

Know Your Audience

Understanding the audience for your visualizations is paramount. Different stakeholders may have varying levels of data literacy and distinct informational needs. To design effective visualizations:

Identify Stakeholder Needs: Engage with end-users to understand what insights they require and how they intend to use the data. Tailor visualizations to meet these needs.

Consider User Proficiency: Assess the data literacy of your audience. For less experienced users, opt for simpler visualizations that avoid jargon and technical complexity.

Customize for Different Roles: Different departments may need specific insights. For instance, a sales team may focus on sales performance metrics, while a finance team may prioritize budget adherence. Design visualizations that cater to these specific needs.

Choose the Right Visualization Type

Selecting the appropriate type of visualization is critical for effective communication. Here are common visualization types and their best uses:

Bar Charts: Ideal for comparing discrete categories, such as sales by region. They are easy to interpret and highlight differences effectively.

Line Charts: Best for showing trends over time, such as monthly revenue growth. They provide clear insights into changes and patterns.

Pie Charts: Useful for displaying parts of a whole, though they should be limited to a small number of categories to avoid confusion. They work well when showing percentage distributions.

Scatter Plots: Effective for illustrating relationships between two variables, allowing for the identification of correlations or outliers.

Heat Maps: Useful for displaying data density and patterns across two dimensions, such as sales performance by region and product category.

Choosing the right visualization type can significantly enhance the clarity and effectiveness of your data presentation.

Simplify Visualizations

Clarity should be the primary goal of any data visualization. Overly complex or cluttered visuals can confuse rather than inform. To simplify your visualizations:

Limit the Number of Elements: Avoid overcrowding visualizations with too much information. Focus on key metrics and insights that drive the narrative.

Use Clear Labels and Titles: Ensure all visualizations have descriptive titles and axis labels. This helps users quickly understand what they are looking at.

Eliminate Unnecessary Elements: Remove gridlines, excessive colors, or decorative elements that do not contribute to the message. Keeping designs clean enhances comprehension.

Employ Effective Color Schemes

Color is a powerful tool in data visualization, influencing how users interpret and engage with the data. To use color effectively:

Choose a Consistent Palette: Establish a cohesive color palette that aligns with organizational branding and enhances the visual appeal. Consistency helps users recognize patterns and themes.

Use Color for Meaning: Assign specific colors to convey meaning, such as using red for negative values and green for positive ones. This practice facilitates quick interpretation of trends and outliers.

Be Mindful of Accessibility: Ensure color choices are accessible to all users, including those with color vision deficiencies. Use contrasting colors and patterns in addition to color to convey information.

Design for Interaction

Interactivity in visualizations can enhance user engagement and enable deeper exploration of data. Both Tableau and Power BI support various interactive features that can improve user experience:

Filters and Slicers: Allow users to filter data based on specific criteria, such as date ranges or categories. This feature empowers users to explore the data that is most relevant to them.

Drill-Down Capabilities: Enable users to click on visual elements to access more detailed information. This interactivity supports exploratory analysis and uncovers insights not immediately visible.

Tooltips: Use tooltips to provide additional context when users hover over data points. This feature can display supplementary information without cluttering the main visualization.

Maintain a Logical Flow

The arrangement of visual elements plays a crucial role in guiding users through the data story. To create a logical flow:

Use a Z-Pattern Layout: Organize visual elements in a Z-pattern, leading the viewer's eye from top left to bottom right. This layout aligns with how most people scan visual information.

Group Related Elements: Place related visualizations close together to create a cohesive narrative. This grouping helps users understand relationships between different data points.

Prioritize Key Insights: Position the most critical metrics prominently to ensure they capture attention. Ensure that secondary metrics are easy to find but do not overshadow primary insights.

Test and Iterate

The design process for data visualizations should be iterative. Testing visualizations with real users can uncover usability issues and areas for improvement:

Gather Feedback: Solicit feedback from stakeholders to assess the effectiveness of visualizations. Use this input to make adjustments that enhance clarity and usability.

Conduct Usability Testing: Observe users as they interact with visualizations to identify pain points or confusion. Use this information to refine designs.

Iterate Based on Insights: Continuously iterate on designs based on feedback and changing user needs. Regular updates can help ensure that visualizations remain relevant and effective.

Document Data Sources and Methodologies

Transparency is essential in data visualization, particularly when it comes to data sources and methodologies. To foster trust and credibility:

Cite Data Sources: Clearly indicate the origins of the data used in visualizations. This transparency helps users understand the context and reliability of the information.

Explain Methodologies: Provide explanations of any calculations or transformations performed on the data. This information can help users evaluate the validity of the insights presented.

Conclusion

Implementing best practices for data visualization in Tableau and Power BI can significantly enhance the clarity, effectiveness, and usability of visual representations. By understanding the audience, selecting appropriate visualization types, simplifying designs, and promoting interactivity, organizations can communicate insights more effectively and support informed decision-making. Regular testing and iteration, combined with transparency regarding data sources and methodologies, further strengthen the credibility and impact of data visualizations. As data continues to play a pivotal role in business strategy, mastering the art of data visualization will be essential for driving success.

Chapter 17: Case Studies: Real-World Applications of Tableau and Power BI

Introduction to Case Studies

Case studies provide valuable insights into how organizations leverage Tableau and Power BI to solve real-world business challenges. By examining specific implementations, we can understand the practical applications of these tools, the strategies employed, and the outcomes achieved. This chapter highlights several case studies across different industries, showcasing the versatility and effectiveness of data visualization in decision-making.

Retail Industry: Enhancing Customer Experience

Company Overview: A leading retail chain sought to improve customer experience and optimize inventory management across its stores.

Challenge: The company faced challenges in understanding customer preferences and managing inventory levels effectively. With multiple data sources, including sales transactions, customer feedback, and inventory levels, the organization struggled to gain a comprehensive view of operations.

Implementation: The retail chain implemented Tableau to create an interactive dashboard that integrated data from various sources. Key features included:

Sales Performance Tracking: Dashboards visualized sales trends by region, product category, and store location. This enabled managers to identify high-performing products and underperforming areas quickly.

Customer Feedback Analysis: The dashboard included sentiment analysis of customer feedback collected from surveys and social media. By visualizing this data, the company could identify areas for improvement and adapt its offerings.

Inventory Optimization: Using historical sales data, the team forecasted future demand for products, helping optimize inventory levels and reduce stockouts.

Outcome: The retail chain achieved a 15% increase in customer satisfaction scores and a 20% reduction in inventory costs within six months of implementing the dashboard. The insights gained led to targeted marketing campaigns and improved product assortment in stores.

Healthcare Industry: Improving Patient Care

Organization Overview: A regional healthcare provider aimed to enhance patient care and operational efficiency in its facilities.

Challenge: The organization needed to monitor key performance indicators (KPIs) related to patient care, including wait times, treatment outcomes, and patient satisfaction. However, data was siloed across departments, making it difficult to derive actionable insights.

Implementation: Power BI was chosen for its robust integration capabilities and user-friendly interface. Key components of the implementation included:

Patient Dashboard: A centralized dashboard provided real-time insights into patient flow, including average wait times and patient demographics. Healthcare providers could monitor patient volumes and allocate resources more effectively.

Quality Metrics Tracking: The dashboard visualized key quality metrics, such as readmission rates and treatment outcomes. This allowed clinical teams to identify trends and implement quality improvement initiatives.

Patient Satisfaction Analysis: Survey data was integrated to analyze patient satisfaction scores, helping identify areas needing attention and improvement.

Outcome: The healthcare provider reduced average wait times by 25% and improved patient satisfaction scores by 30% within a year. Enhanced visibility into patient care processes facilitated data-driven decisions that directly impacted patient outcomes.

Financial Services: Streamlining Reporting Processes

Company Overview: A global financial services firm sought to streamline its reporting processes and enhance data accuracy across departments.

Challenge: The organization struggled with manual reporting methods that were time-consuming and prone to errors. Different teams used disparate systems, leading to inconsistencies in financial data.

Implementation: The firm adopted Tableau for its powerful data visualization capabilities and ability to connect to multiple data sources seamlessly. Key implementation steps included:

Automated Reporting: Dashboards were created to automate the generation of key financial reports, such as profit and loss statements and budget vs. actual analyses. This reduced the time spent on manual data aggregation.

Real-Time Insights: The organization implemented live data connections to enable real-time tracking of financial performance metrics. Stakeholders could access up-to-date information at any time.

Cross-Departmental Collaboration: Interactive dashboards facilitated collaboration among departments by providing a shared view of financial data. This transparency improved communication and alignment on financial goals.

Outcome: The financial services firm reduced reporting time by 50%, allowing teams to focus on strategic analysis rather than data entry. The enhanced accuracy of financial data led to more informed decision-making and better compliance with regulatory requirements.

Manufacturing Industry: Optimizing Production Processes

Company Overview: A manufacturing company aimed to enhance operational efficiency and reduce production downtime across its facilities.

Challenge: The company faced challenges in monitoring machine performance and production metrics, leading to inefficiencies and unexpected downtimes.

Implementation: Power BI was selected to create dashboards that visualized production data from various machines and processes. Key features included:

Machine Performance Monitoring: Dashboards tracked machine utilization rates, downtime occurrences, and maintenance schedules. This visibility allowed operators to identify issues quickly and take corrective actions.

Production KPIs: Key performance indicators such as cycle time, throughput, and defect rates were visualized, enabling managers to monitor production efficiency in real time.

Predictive Maintenance: The team implemented predictive analytics to forecast equipment failures based on historical data. This proactive approach minimized unplanned downtimes and maintenance costs.

Outcome: The manufacturing company achieved a 30% reduction in production downtime and a 15% increase in overall equipment effectiveness (OEE) within a year. Enhanced visibility into production processes empowered teams to optimize operations and implement continuous improvement initiatives.

Education Sector: Enhancing Student Outcomes

Institution Overview: A university aimed to improve student performance and retention rates by leveraging data analytics.

Challenge: The university needed to analyze student data, including academic performance, engagement metrics, and retention rates, to identify at-risk students and implement intervention strategies.

Implementation: The university adopted Tableau to create an interactive dashboard that integrated data from various sources, including academic records and student engagement platforms. Key implementation features included:

Student Performance Dashboards: Visualizations tracked student grades, attendance, and engagement levels. Advisors could identify students at risk of falling behind and offer timely support.

Engagement Analysis: The dashboard visualized participation in extracurricular activities and events, helping the university understand factors influencing student engagement and retention.

Predictive Analytics for Retention: By analyzing historical data, the university developed predictive models to identify students likely to drop out. This proactive approach allowed for targeted interventions.

Outcome: The university improved student retention rates by 20% and increased overall student satisfaction scores. Data-driven interventions empowered academic advisors to provide timely support, ultimately enhancing student outcomes.

Conclusion

These case studies illustrate the transformative impact of Tableau and Power BI across various industries. By effectively leveraging data visualization tools, organizations can enhance decision-making, improve operational efficiency, and drive better outcomes. The ability to analyze and visualize data empowers teams to identify trends, streamline processes, and address challenges proactively. As data continues to grow in importance, these tools will remain essential for organizations seeking to harness the full potential of their data.